MW00896106
Facing
Fear with
Faith

When two of the leading laypersons of our country come to our aid in facing the United States' most cutting tragedy, we are fortunate. If we give them the time and come with them to rest in contemplation on the bedrock of our faith we will know a new hope, realizing we are embraced by an eternal love. Poetry and prayer—"a way to truly experience my dependence on God."

—M. Basil Pennington, O.C.S.O.

On September 11, 2001, all of us—even and especially believing Christians—were cast across a new threshold into the realm of "terrorism" and "prolonged insecurity." Jones and Leckey have composed a contemplative dwelling place—furnished with poetry and Spirited conversation—for the ongoing formation of souls who seek Christian bedrock, who long for a deeper faithfulness in a world forever changed, and who are open to making the hard journey from fear to faith, terror to trust, stress to security, horror to hope, grief to generosity, and loss into a yet greater love.

—Sharon Daloz Parks
Coauthor, *Common Fire: Leading Lives of Commitment in a Complex World*

Has the familiar path of your faith been obscured by the events of September 11, 2001? Enter the pages of this richly provisioned book and let its companionable yet challenging wisdom help you find wellsprings of quiet, courageous peace—a peace so desperately needed in our anxious, disoriented times.

—John S. Mogabgab
Editor, *Weavings*

Facing Fear with Faith

Arthur Jones and Dolores Leckey

– An RCL Company –
Allen, Texas

Acknowledgments

The Scripture quotations contained herein are from the *New Revised Standard Version Bible: Catholic Edition* copyright © 1993 and 1989 by the Division of Christian Education for the National Council of the Churches of Christ in the U.S.A. Used by permission. All rights reserved.

Send all inquiries to:
Thomas More® Publishing
An RCL Company
200 East Bethany Drive
Allen, Texas 75002-3804

Telephone: 800-264-0368 / 972-390-6300
Fax: 800-688-8356 / 972-390-6560

Visit us at: **www.thomasmore.com**
Customer Service E-mail: **cservice@rcl-enterprises.com**

Printed in the United States of America

7486 ISBN 88347-486-7

1 2 3 4 5 06 05 04 03 02

Dedication

This book is enhallowed by the people and priests, living and dead, of the faith community that is Our Lady Queen of Peace in Arlington, Virginia.

It is dedicated to our grandchildren: Tyler and Sarah Jones, Samuel Xavier Brase, Roman and Maria Leckey, Cameron and Conor Marcellus, and Monica and Grace Marie Leckey.

Contents

Introduction

Arthur writes:

I work from home. Very early on the morning of September 11, 2001 (West Coast time—I live in Los Angeles County), I dropped my wife off at the curb at LAX for her flight to Washington Dulles. We kissed and I drove the hour or more through the tortuous traffic back to the house.

I'd been home barely ten minutes when she called—all planes canceled. She would try to get to Burbank Airport and call me from there to collect her.

I turned on the television and watched what the entire world watched. I said a silent prayer, perhaps more than one. And I did a quick mental check: where are our children? I knew my wife wasn't in the air. Nor was the son who flies most. He was on the West Coast of Ireland with his sister. My other son in California had not yet left for work.

I didn't have to say thank you to God. I oozed it. Gratitude emanated from my pores.

Two mornings later, I was in a Catholic high school listening to a class on peace-making cope with what happened to the extent that anyone could, teens or not. The next week, I was at an Afghan radio station in Los Angeles to find out how they were faring.

As the first days turned into the first weeks, I was doing what nearly everyone else was doing—working my way through it. At one level, but not the deeper level. During a chance telephone call with my friend Jim Srodes in Washington, as we talked about an entirely different topic, he suggested out of the blue that I write a book on facing terrorism with faith. I drafted an outline, called John Sprague at Thomas More, he agreed. Within three days, Dolores had agreed to co-author it with me.

Dolores writes:
I awoke on September 11 full of anticipation. This was the day I was having a reproduction of a fresco from Priscilla's catacombs, a mural, installed in my home. The catacombs of Priscilla are a favorite place of mine, a place of quiet and respite in the busy city of Rome.

Maybe it's because those catacombs—the place—is the home of a second-century Roman matron who ran a household, welcomed guests, no doubt worried about her children (and husband)—and who happened to be a Christian. The lower reaches of Priscilla's home are scenes of beauty. One wall depicts a small group sitting at a table. They appear to be mostly women.

There is bread, a cup (of wine perhaps), and baskets on the floor. It is called "The Breaking of the Bread." The colors (sepia and blue) and the composition of people gathered in friendship and hope convey an aura of peace.

At 8:30 A.M. the installers arrived, laid out the canvas that would cover a wall (so that it would look as if it was painted on the wall), and began all the other details of the task. I found myself talking to Priscilla.

About 8:55 my phone rang. My daughter Celia, who lives quite close to the Pentagon, breathlessly asked if we were all right. "Of course." Then she told me about New York (where

> my husband and I grew up). The TV was now on and the installers and we stared in disbelief at the frightening images. Celia called again, in tears. Her small cottage was rattling from the Pentagon explosion and she said another plane was headed toward Washington. She was going to the nearby high school to see her son.
>
> Forty minutes later she was sitting with us sipping water. (I've always thought that water was good in times of stress.) She had walked the mile and a half to the school to check on Sam, and then on to our home. She had intended to drive but a national guardsman on a bike cautioned her to stay off the road. The installers tried to call their homes but the lines were busy. I tried to call family in New York City, but there was only an automatic message available: "Due to an emergency your call cannot be completed."
>
> And so it was for the next week.
>
> By noon, "The Breaking of the Bread" had been installed and fighter planes could be heard in the sky above. Only Christ could make sense of such contradictions.

What happened to our country and to ourselves on September 11, 2001, was that our fates, and our states of "being," were brutally, fiendishly, altered.

The early feelings included feelings of helplessness, helplessness mixed with anger. As our emotions dealt with these reactions, and thought set in, the second wave of feelings—as our vulnerability was made plain to us—included shafts of fear, even momentary terror.

Now we have this entire mix of muted anger, of wanting to get on with life, of fear for others and ourselves, yet the knowledge that everything has changed, without being quite certain what actually has changed. This book is less about what precisely has changed than it is about dealing with that other, flowing, turbulent swirl of mixed emotions, feelings, and responses.

As Catholic Christians, we know we can counteract the feeling that our future is being altered against our will by changing ourselves to outpace those who would change us.

To change ourselves to face fear requires a journeying into deeper, easier—even happier, or at least more comfortably resigned and trusting—reliance on God.

The starting point, as it must be, is with poetry. Within minutes, or days, of that dreadful September 11 moment, the poets were already at work to show us—as Christians and as Americans—who we are or could be. They forged their verse in the fire, dust, and tumbling deaths.

Incense

—For Those Lost

Twin pillars of smoke rise
from the pyre. Dreams
they drift to heaven.
Incense for the baptism
of the new world order.
Incensed, we've no object
for our anger.

Souls set free soar
above the altar
of their senseless nativity
and unite in their ascension
blessing the efforts,
sanctifying the response.
—Dennis Queally

12 September 2001

In Houston, Texas, hundreds of miles away geographically from Dennis Queally in North Bergen, New Jersey, Cheryl Sawyer took us inside what Queally had described from the outside:

One

As the soot and dirt and ash rained down,
We became one color.

As we carried each other down the stairs of the
burning building,
We became one class.

As we lit candles of waiting and hope,
We became one generation.

As the firefighters and police officers fought their
way into the inferno,
We became one gender.

As we fell to our knees in prayer for strength,
We became one faith.

As we whispered or shouted words of encouragement,
We spoke one language.

As we gave our blood in lines a mile long,
We became one body.

As we mourned together the great loss,
We became one family.

As we cried tears of grief and loss,
We became one soul.

As we retell with pride of the sacrifice of heroes,
We become one people.

We are . . .
One color

One class
One generation
One gender
One faith
One language
One body
One family
One soul
One people
We are
The Power of One.
One Nation, Under God, Indivisible.
We are United.
We are America.
—Cheryl Sawyer

In Cheryl Sawyer's poetry, the unifying element of our "one nation under God" is clearly expressed. It is an ideal en route to reality.

There are two other realities—one secular, concerning us as Americans; the other religious and spiritual that concerns us as Catholics.

The secular reality is that our fates, our states of 'being,' have been altered before.

As the television images repeated what was happening over and over again, we could join with a U.S. Army sergeant who said more than fifty years earlier: "I don't even want to think of what the sight of all these terrible things is doing to me." He knew that what he was seeing was scarring his psyche—he was looking at a concentration camp in Germany.

"How can I ever have the tenderness to worry about your scratched finger," he wrote, "or the other little things which will now seem so insignificant to me?"

These sentiments belonged to all of us at some point after the images were etched into our reality. We have faced questions like these in the hours and days after the airplanes with their fated human cargoes were callously turned into flying bombs, into killing machines turned on their fellow men and women. Before our eyes!

We feel the need to cry out, but at what?

Loud and Quiet

I'm mad as anything
I want nothing more
Than to yell as loud as thunder
Yet I keep as quiet as a snowfall
—M. Tufano

When terrorists cruelly and callously ripped the lives and heart out of lower Manhattan, they ripped from all of us Americans, individually and collectively, our sense of personal and national security. It is equally true that we are faced with death—with the threat of death—in a new way. Death as the angry, deliberate where-might-it-strike-next unseen yet unflagging presence. Our national commentators, even the most prominent in the land, have said: "We are forever changed." "Things will never be the same again." We simply do not know what might be coming.

For Americans everything has altered, particularly our belief that life somehow was meant to be predictable, in more or less a straight line. Certainly, everything has changed from what we were experiencing on September 10, 2001.

So yes, we can acknowledge our fates have been dramatically altered. But predictable is not what life is. Nor ever was.

Hence, one element of this book—the immediate questions:

- What has changed?
- What has gone before that applies?

Then there's the other element—meaning and faith.

- What does the reality of September 11, 2001, mean to us as Christians?
- Where does religious faith fit in?
- What ought this tragedy do to our life and work as Christians?
- Has September 11 jarred our faith, jolted us out of complacency, called on us to plumb our depths, required us to more clearly define our Christian gifts and charisms?

We believe that it has.

Questions are asked here about the peaks and valleys of the rugged terrain that is our immediate psychological and spiritual life and post-September 11 state of being. We're charting our bewilderment as our implied questions confront Terror and Fear, and seek sense, succor, and solace in Prayer, Sacred Writings, Quiet Calm, Perseverance, Beauty, and Life Beyond Death.

The themes are woven through seven chapters:

1. Moving Beyond Fear,
2. Facing Fear with Faith,
3. Facing Fear with Hope,
4. Facing Fear with Love,
5. Facing Fear as Family and Community,
6. Facing Fear with Prayer,
7. Facing Fear with Contemplation.

The style of this book is conversational. The alternating voices of Dolores and Arthur are offered as companionship along the way. Think of the poetry as medieval chapels-of-ease, stopping places for rest and reflection.

The book asks if in all our pondering we can genuinely change for the better our philosophy of life, which for Christians is a fancy phrase for how deep is our relationship with God, how centered is our life and our prayer life on what matters most.

We have to rely on something, someone:

Trust

No safety nets lie
under this tightrope.
If we stumble
the air holds us.
We can misstep
but not fall—not unless
we reject the air
around us,
the God who is all.

The acrobat
doesn't struggle
but relaxes,
lets her toes
sense the path
along the wire.
Her body braces
in the wind,
taut but flexible.

That lizard
with the spiked tail,
that lizard that bites
and won't let go.
Surrender to its message.

The desert dries everything
but evening cools
as we crawl along

and cardinals
occasionally fly
into our paths.
—Stella Nesanovich

The hope is that, prompted and pursued by September 11, we can reach into what constitutes our self-identity as individuals and believers and, while rummaging around in there, reestablish our Christian bedrock. First by locating it, next by shoveling off the rubble, then by brushing it off so we can better see its symmetry and flow, and finally by finding a place to sit and rest on this bedrock in contemplation.

Nothing to do with God and belief—once one has accepted the gift of faith—comes easy.

Simple Faith

If He be Father
Then I be son or daughter

If She be creator
Then I be Her work of art

If God be love
Then I be-loved
—Joseph W. Mayer

Reidentifying the bedrock of our beliefs is work—honest work, but hard work. It requires a passion, the energy of a compassionate heart that wants to reach in, in order to reach out. It is costly; it demands time—time we have to take from something else. It requires allowing our search to preoccupy us a little—how else can we think about ourselves and God in the corridors of faith, hope, charity, beauty, and contemplation, unless we let the thoughts permeate our every day? All belief is a work in progress.

What we're proposing here is to add fresh motivation and commitment to a progress that may not be geared to the anxieties around our daily lives. Not everyone will find reassurance in the statement that sometimes the best thing for us to do is just to stop, and sit. And not even think.

In the journey that is this book—as we walk and talk about faith, hope, and charity, about family, community, prayer, and contemplation all squaring off against fear—we need comfortable mental walking shoes. We need good companions and a measure of hope. Prayer and poetry are those comfortable shoes. Fellow human beings alive on September 11, and born every day since, are the companions. The measure of hope is our concentration on attempting to see life afresh at every fresh moment. As we walk along, we are reacquainting ourselves with what we believe, the beliefs we have and haven't questioned, the practices we've meant to implement, and perhaps neglected.

Along the way, we regularly stop for a moment here and there. It's reflection. It's as if we'd come across that medieval wayside chapel-of-ease. For in times of stress and uncertainty, even the believer doesn't always know where to begin, or how to go on. Even believers sometimes must rest awhile.

For some of us, this journey means a new search is on for the meaning of life.

For others, it is searching more deeply for the meaningful God.

The God of the major metropolitan area with its congested streets, constant busyness, and cathedrals.

I walk along a busy street
The usual crowds are everywhere
And I look at them—to my astonishment
In a strangely different kind of way today.
—Anthony de Mello, S.J.

The God of the ordered suburbs and their trim corner churches.

Exit 92B

I haunt the suburbs, life without end
Passionate visitor, nights and weekend,
Heart's where the home is, where I'm alive.
House, spouse, and kids off I-95.
When life's a commute, a book on tape.
Exit 92B: my God-given escape.
—John Sladen Whittle

The God of the rural areas and little chapels and houses of worship.

Crossroads

Twenty houses. Thirty-two, if trailers count.
Full gospel, tin roof. No gas station now.
The black-white sign on leaving
Said "Come back soon."
A town away the black-white sign
Said "Mass at 9 and noon."
—Alice Ward

The God who needs no buildings.

In April Once

In April once
We walked the cowpath bordered
With cedars.
Earth still damp from late thaws
Sun-warmed mud
On bare feet (and paws) we came out

To an overgrown field (no gate)
Fine bird cover—the air very quiet
"Where's the woodcock?" I asked.
"Sh-h-h," said my father. "Wait."
—Adapted from Hope Sawyer Buyukmihci

The God who knows the cry of pain, and death.

Reversals and Recent Acts of God
For Father Oscar S. Vasquez-Munoz,
Ordained May 18, 1991, Lake Charles, Louisiana
Died June 18, 1991, Bogotá, Colombia

One month after you lay face down
on our cathedral floor, you died
far away in your homeland hospital
for lack of a respirator.
"He died in a country of trouble,"
wag tongues with little taste
for holiness.

The morning you died in Bogota,
lightning struck us in Louisiana,
The cathedral bells rang randomly
for an hour. No one could figure
out their electronic brain.
Next door the Court House asked,
"Can no one reverse
this latest act of God?"
The bells have heavy tongues
yet beyond the metal rim
of time are soundless.
The ordination you delayed

to be fluent has passed—
no need for words now.

In your native land,
you are laid out, face up,
eyes closed to us and
covered with the earth
you came from, earth richer
now for your passage,
but facing the heavens
you came among us
as missionary to open.
—Leo Luke Marcello

The God, too, of the country's physical majesty—the magnificent mountain vistas, the calming waterways—and those who dwell therein.

Pure Air

Pure air, morning song
Rising Sun constitute
Our Trinity of peace
—Vic Hummert

The God of each flower and leaf and rock. The God of the tidal pool and the life that inhabits it. The God in the things made by human hands—the beautifully styled object, the painting whose meaning changes with each viewing. The God in the descriptive passage, the ceramic bowl, the whetstone, the kind word, the compassionate hand, the understanding face.

Meanwhile, continuing on through this book means we are on a pilgrimage of joy, not penance. Our conversation and thinking is focused on making decisions. We are thinking how we might take the risk of being a more "present" us than in the past, and offering a slightly different "presence" to those who know us. We need to be their anchor in the face of terror, their stability when fear threatens to engulf, their place to turn when anxiety seems to be the only emotional outlet.

If we can be these things to people who turn to us, we discover we are these same things to ourselves. We know in advance that this is so—but the reality doesn't strike us until it happens.

In essence, we can redefine our Christian identity—not change it, not artificially pretty it up—but renew it, draw it with bolder pen strokes in stronger lines. As Atlanta Archbishop Paul Hallinan (1911–1968) once asked rhetorically: "Why do our worship and our meditation need renewal? Because we offer God a routine mind."

The actual, if sometimes subterranean, content of our spiritual and religious and philosophical makeup is there all the time, waiting to be reformulated. Renewed, it can handle the demands we hadn't anticipated we'd have to make on it.

As we reflect on what happened because of those viciously inspired tragedies of September 11, 2001, we can draw from our religious and spiritual and experiential niches, nooks, and crannies a clearer understanding of our thought patterns. And, looking at those thought patterns—the collected curios of our self-identity storehouse—we can reshape how we approach life. Life by the minute, by the hour, by the day. We can help others. Help directly if we're asked, or by example if we're not.

We can reorder our belief life in order to face fear. We can face the continuing and real aftermath of terror—and new terrors threatened.

In all this reshaping we live a new awareness of life to the full.

Burning

I think of Hopkins burning all his poetry,
the leaping flames in the fireplace,

his words, his thoughts in smoke, the look on his face
to see gray ashes in the orange glow.
I wonder, did he weep, and did he know
that he would ever write again, and grace
would find him, even in his lonely place
where all the winds of winter seemed to blow?
How could he know the warm breast of Holy Ghost
would find the poet there and offer him
bright wings, and in the dawn windhover Host
would come in blazing light, compelling him
to praise with voice the One who dwells inmost
and gives us then that gift, his resonant hymn?
—Nancy J. Nowak

From the burning we watched, the poetry of our previous, seemingly secure lives tossed into the flames of the World Trade Center, we can emerge on the warm breast of Holy Ghost—the image of realistic Christian calmness. The calmness that comes from the faith, hope, love, and courageous facing of terror and fear. Terror anticipated, terror met, and fear overcome.

We can avoid being consumed by terrorist created anxieties. We can face each minute, each hour, each day.

We do it through the joy of this journey. The joy of seeing God anew and afresh in each other. God anew and fresh in ourselves.

Welcome to our pilgrimage. Welcome to the poetry, the chapels-of-ease along the way.

—Arthur Jones and Dolores Leckey

1

Moving Beyond Fear

In any nation that calls itself religious, the Church must provide the vision of what society should be. Our first task is to save our souls. But we cannot save them in heaven, nor in the sanctuary. We can only save them . . . in the world in which we live.

—Archbishop Paul Hallinan

Because of what has happened in America, because of the tragic events of September 11, 2001, something different is being asked of all of us—as Americans, as believers, as spiritually inclined human beings, and as people of specific faiths. We are facing questions that can neither be avoided nor postponed.

Priest-psychologist Henri Nouwen (d. 1996) could have been speaking about the past few months when he wrote: "The past few years, all ask for a new way to speak about God. This new way includes not only content, but form. Not only what I say, but also how I say it, should be different."

Not only what we believe about life, but how we now live life should be different. The requirement: to develop a new way to reflect, to speak, to act about God, about life, personally and in community. Because of September 11. But also because we should anyway, as if September 11 had never occurred.

We can become more contemplative. "The eyes of the contemplative see into the very depths," said French theologian Jean Danielou (d. 1974), "whereas our eyes go no further than the surface."

We can we look in places we've never looked before—especially within ourselves. We can look everywhere. We can be a little like Emily Dickinson: "Not knowing when the dawn will come, I open every door."

We can open every door leading into and out of the storehouse of our collected life, including our collected Christian life. We can clear the shelves in the antiques shop we've built from our notions and experiences, our happenstance philosophy of spirituality, and in so doing adjust to this newer, more apparently threatening reality.

What sort of questions clear our shelves? Questions like those implied by Saint Polycarp (d. 155) when he urged Christians in the second century to "toil together, suffer together, rest together, and rise together." Questions about not worrying so much where precisely we are headed, but rather, committing ourselves to the journey—in trust.

Following Directions

In all the mysteries
Surrounding life
On this planet
Our reluctance
To ask directions
When we lose our way
Is among the
Most confusing

And it is not just
The male of the species

Who tries to fake it
By pretending all along
That the destination
Is just around
The corner

Even when trying to find
A mall or an arena
Where we want to be
We tough it out
And if we do find our way
It is usually unintentionally
And not by design

But to gamble
With directions
To the Kingdom
Or to take the wrong turns
Because we don't ask
Is at best
Mind-boggling
And at the least
Mindless

For the Master's road
Is relatively simple
Though never easy
And since it means
Traveling with One
Who is the Way
We never arrive
By accident.
—Father Michael J. Kennedy

Can we self-examine even our uncertainties so that our response is a fresh, personal philosophy quite unlike our pre-September 11 philosophy? A philosophy more true to who and what we've always wanted to be?

We have much to draw on—most particularly the first few centuries of Christianity, and the solidity of the monastic and contemplative experience.

If we belong to a faith community, we have an immediate source of strength—each other, but each other in a different dimension—the one we call "communion." The community that is the Eucharist.

What did it take, in the face of fear, for those original Christians to hold together in those first few hundred years? Surely the Eucharist and Jesus' words were the twin centers then, as now.

The essence of the early Christian community was that for almost four centuries, despite torture, despite death, despite being hunted and hounded and hated, despite every provocation, they maintained an unshakable belief in peace, in prayer, in service, and in nonviolent response. The early Christians were brutalized—they never became terrorists. They were crucified—they never organized as a guerrilla band seeking reprisals. They cared for the widows and orphans; they cared for the sick and buried the dead—and not just their own.

It was this aspect of their lives—how they lived each minute, each hour, and each day in Jesus' peace, in service to others—that anchored the faith and caused it to spread. Christianity spread so successfully and so serenely, its anchorage was so strong, that Emperor Constantine usurped it by adopting it and making it an instrument of the state. He had seen its strength. And now, again, must we.

Philosopher Rodger Beehler says that "if human beings did not care about one another there could not be what we speak of as morality, for the reason that morality is a manifestation of that caring."

The caring can come in a simple way by telling others what we ourselves are told. For example, in his book *Landscapes of Fear*

(Pantheon, New York, 1979), Yi-fu Tuan describes fear as "a complex feeling in which two strains, alarm and anxiety, are clearly distinguishable. Alarm is triggered by an obtrusive event in the environment; an instinctive response is to combat it or run. Anxiety, on the other hand, is a diffuse sense of dread and presupposes an ability to anticipate." We feel these things and we hear the Christian antidote that is always present:

Be not afraid
I go before you always
Come, follow me,
For I will give you rest.
—Bob Dufford, S.J.

This enables us to say to others—be not afraid, I am with you always. Come, follow him, and he will give us both rest. This lateral thinking suggests that the community of saints is everyone around us, and that we must banish some preconceived notions. We'll be looking at both the community and the notions as we go along.

Similarly, we are called, as we reflect deeper, to rethink who and what we are personally as Christians. We bolster our defenses against fear and terror by removing those defenses altogether. We look at these same things through the eyes of those who know no faith, no certainty. Then—and we shall do it once more later on—we look at these matters through the eyes of those who have known much fear.

A psychologist who describes himself as "still searching" gets to the nub of this issue when he writes that faith/religion "provides a response—maybe the only plausible response to fear. But it seems that this begs many questions. Does faith simply give us the best ending possible in impossible circumstances? That is, we die in contact with the divine ground, which may be better than dying in spiritual emptiness. Or, does faith empower us?"

We take God's grace where we find it. And we receive it even if we don't notice the gift.

The terrorists, for instance, would have Americans running for cover, diving into foxholes of their own making. And that word, "foxholes," provides two immediate and familiar sayings. One, attributed to many people, is: "There are no atheists in foxholes." Then Bishop Fulton J. Sheen (d. 1979) described an atheist as "a man with no invisible means of support."

And yet . . . God is big. God supports atheists through friends. God may support us through our atheist friends.

Walking Through Paradise with a Friend Who Doesn't Believe

At the end of the path you expect nothing,
a clearing perhaps and then pure air,
no trace of animal droppings, insect bites,
just an opening in the trees,
an end of the path cleared before us,
a suddenly treeless empty plain,
not even the sounds of the birds chirping.

Here is the story you desire.
There will be no suffering, no cross.
Everyone you love will feel good.
Around each neck is a chain with a rock,
instead of that man on a cross.
You would celebrate the caves of birth.

For me there are rocks and blood,
nails and broken bones, but I am not
alone in this. We are all within
this one suffering body of life, Christ,
so long as we breathe, but
there is a window, a clearing,
an opening in the wall,

a way out of the cave.
Someone has shown us the opening
by passing through it first
and now calls us along this way.

I will meet you in that clearing, friend.
Whatever we go through, we'll go through.
We will sing together in Paradise
where we have begun to sing even now.
—Leo Luke Marcello

Dominican Sister Maureen Cannon, a campus minister, remembers how when World War II began people packed the churches to pray; they were seeking something. Students flocked in with the rest. This did not happen to the same extent after September 11, she said. It suggests that, in making a decision and division between spirituality and faith, the students were pulling on their spiritual reserves in a time of crisis, perhaps, but not going to church to tap into their faith resources.

Yet God supports constantly. We know not how. We know not where. But for those of us who do think in these faith community terms, the challenge is to be alive to it. God shapes the world *for us* sometimes. Sometimes, God even bends the lightning off course. Simply because we are who we are and God wants us here a moment more for God's reasons.

That the Bones You Have Crushed May Thrill

A great Being of Power was traveling
through the sky
his foot was on a kind of lightning
as a wheel is on a rail, it was his pathway.

The lightning was made entirely
of the spirits of innumerable people close to

one another
and I was one.

He moved in a straight line
and each part of the streak or flash
came into its short conscious existence only
that he
might travel.

I seemed to be directly under the foot of God
and I thought he was grinding his own life
up out of my pain.

Then I saw
that what he had been trying with all his
might to do
was to change the course
to bend the line of lightning to which he was
tied
in the direction in which he wanted to go.

I felt my flexibility, and helplessness
and knew that he would succeed.
He bended me
turning his corner by means of my hurt
hurting me more than I had ever been hurt
in my life, and at the acutest point of this
as he passed I saw.

I understood for a moment things
I have now forgotten
things that no one could remember
while retaining sanity.

The angle was an obtuse angle, and I
remember
thinking

as I woke, that had he made it an acute
or right angle
I should have both suffered and 'seen' still
More
and probably died.
—Judith Robbins

If life is to be lived by the minute and by the hour and by the day—and it is—what needs to change is what we expect from the minute, the hour, and the day.

We get help from unexpected quarters. Ursuline Sister Pascal Conforti is a pastoral and spiritual caregiver at St. Clare's Hospital in Manhattan. After the World Trade Center attack, her ninety-three-year-old mother called her from Buffalo to remind her to be "very careful when you go out." Pascal told her, "You know, Mom, all those people who went to work at the World Trade Center—they were being very, very careful."

"So there is," Sister Pascal tells us, "something about being aware of the situation but not being trapped into thinking that if you are careful enough nothing will happen. This illusion we have of invulnerability," she says, "was very much affronted by the World Trade Center."

She feels there is some way of centering one's self in the moment, connecting in some way with God so that we can set out, and simply pay attention, moment to moment, to what is happening in our interactions with people as we do what we need to do. "And that's about it," she says.

She is quick to point to where she gets some of her quiet calm: "I am dealing with people who—including the World Trade Center attack—over the years have always been coming face-to-face with mortality." (She ministers to both hospital patients and staff.) "So it's been a real revelation for me—even though these are not necessarily folks who spend a lot of time in church, or are educated in a formal way—yet they seem sometimes to have a better sense of what the Christian, Catholic faith is all about. All about, that is, in terms of the cycles of living and dying."

It is the familiar Christian paradox in operation—those who are living on the margins of life are somehow more attuned to the immediate that we are now stretching and changing ourselves to reach for and live in—the God-given moment, minute, hour, and day.

Sister Pascal explains: "There's a way in which, when Jesus talks about, 'you have to be poor to understand what I'm saying—poor in Spirit'—these folks I'm meeting and getting to know often have a more immediate experience of God. Or of Providence or an ever-present transcendent entity or force." They have it, she believes, because the experience has not been mediated out of them by a poor theology, perhaps, or by poor explanations of what can't be explained. And it hasn't been subsumed under the diversions of affluence, because the pressures of just getting through the day are so ever-present.

We need to live in and for the moment. We need to see that life is full, almost complete in itself, in the next momentary exchange, in our constant interactions with people—interactions in person, on the telephone, by e-mail, by letter. All this seeking for a new ease, a bubbling freshness that life is the immediate NOW, really does require that we reacquaint ourselves with what we believe.

None of these steps are necessarily easy—but these aren't simple times. Danger and uncertainty are real. The immediate and medium-term future is one of complexity, some confusion, and a continuing level of anxiety. An anxiety that beeps away at us like one of those monitors at a hospital bedside.

Arthur writes:

Since high school, or perhaps college, we have taken the contents of our self-identity storehouse more or less for granted. Like an antique shop proprietor who picks up items she likes for her antique shop over the years, we simply add to our storehouse from our experience as we go along. Her shop window reflects her likes and dislikes. Her likes she prices higher; her dislikes we see in the sales bin.

Our starting point at this moment is not our religion, but us—me, you—at this moment. Who am I? What do I believe? What do I believe so strongly that others can find shelter in it along with me, as if under the shade of some Mother Tree in the forest? And having rested in such shade, who am I that I can go out again and live my full life knowing life's tenuousness?

In the Light of My Father's Shadow

Standing at the altar
held and upheld by pieces of hearts
that have fashioned my own,
voice strong—words clear, controlled, concise.
"He was so proud," they all said,
and so he should have been—
after all,
I live his life, the life he always wanted, but. . . .

That's all over now,
my life is mine—or is it? Even now?—
a middle-aged man whose life has lost its former familiarity,
its predictability.

I walk unsteady,
unsure,
looking for the meaning of my life.
Why am I here?
Where am I going?
What do YOU want?
Will I ever grow up?

The response comes:
What do you want?

It's not supposed to be like this—
a little boy lost—
but a constant, barely perceptible whisper within me says,
"Walk through this wasteland."
Perhaps, someday, this wilderness will reveals its blessing
buried, deep within,
waiting to be received.

I watch the coffin making its descent—
his shadow gone;
only his sadness remains
in me
his only son
his greatest blessing
his dream now my only reality.
—Father Dan Rocheleau

The life-and-death cycle is more present now. To cope we have to dig up our beliefs, habits, passions, and thought patterns and look at them—to give them a fancy collective title: our philosophy. The English Catholic writer Gilbert K. Chesterton (1874–1936) makes the point (his light-hearted tongue in his quite profound cheek): "Unless a man has a philosophy certain horrible things will happen to him. A man who refuses to have his own philosophy will have only the used-up scraps of somebody else's philosophy."

Archbishop Paul Hallinan, reflecting on the prevalence of the lack of a personal philosophy, said: "Much of our modern conversation is merely an exchange of assorted prejudices. What passes for thought is only a search for the newspaper or magazine which agrees with one's likes and dislikes."

Many centuries before G. K. Chesterton and Archbishop Hallinan, the African bishop and saint Cyprian (d. 258) tied together the two thoughts—philosophy and action—in a way that directly affects us. Saint Cyprian's Christian community was poor and uneducated but rich in other ways for he said: "We are philosophers not in word, but in act; we do not say great things, but we do live them."

Like that early Christian community, we need to know the great things in order to live them. And many of those great things, simply expressed, have been engulfed by the materialism, affluence, and busyness of the lives we have developed, as a nation, as a community, as individuals.

Father Nouwen's words combine Archbishop Hallinan's theme and Chesterton's thoughts to remind us that the tragic events of September 11 demand a "human heart [that] searches for something greater than its own pettiness."

We're more apt to see the human heart closed off and exhibiting its own pettiness. A colleague reports that on September 12 she pulled into her slot at the university parking lot, and saw two students headed toward a vacant spot. One was going the correct way, the other going the wrong way down a one-way lane. The student going the correct way got there first and parked. The other one leapt from her car, screaming abuse and threatening physical violence. It became so threatening that campus security was called.

The previous day, several thousand people had had their lives snatched from them. The screaming, unyielding woman in the parking lot had probably cried watching it all on television. The message, obviously, had not registered. Or had it? Was the individual incapable of getting the message? Was the individual so disturbed by the events of September 11 that simple miscues took on exaggerated proportions? Or had the individual simply become inured to social calamities and this was her "normal" personality at its aggressive worst?

Henri Nouwen probes the idea of moving beyond who and where we are now. Henri Nouwen was a writer. He used his writing to further his point about revival, about rethinking. We can jettison some of what was in the past, or we can simply move on from it. "Many of my books," he wrote late in life, "no longer express my spiritual vision and, although I am not dismissing my earlier writing as no longer valid, I feel that something different is being asked of me."

Different things now are being asked of us.

Dolores writes:

I write this on the eve of the feast of Saint Therese of Lisieux, the most recent Doctor of the Church—the feast is October 1.

Saint Therese received this prestigious title for her doctrine, which is not some kind of "riff" on Thomistic philosophy, or some explication of the intricacies of the mystical life. No. Her doctrine has been known as "the Little Way." Simply stated, it means that surrender to God (not personal achievement) is the essence of the spiritual life.

She describes our life as one of children in relationship to a loving parent, and this includes trust and dependency. In terms of behavior, it relates to the smallest actions one can do, in the circumstances of everyday life, for the glory of God.

There are stories of Saint Therese picking up pins dropped on the convent floor, and offering them up for special intentions. These are the dynamics of everyday life that all of us can relate to.

When the daily stories of firefighters and police struggling with the debris of the World Trace Center filled the airwaves, Therese came to mind. The stories described men and women from distant places across the United States who were moved to travel to New York City to help the rescue operation. Sometimes they waited for some task to be assigned. Therese's "Little Way" loomed up for those of us at home, stricken and wanting to help. We could perform small acts of service and join them, in prayer, to the on-site efforts.

We could pick up trash and offer our efforts in prayer for the rescue workers faced with much more daunting work. We could simply engage in the duties that are ours, remembering the ongoing duty of the rescue workers.

Saint Therese inspires meditation on the meaning of surrender. Clearly the fellowship of AA practices this, but there are also stories of others—leaders—who entered into this dynamic of surrender to God and there found the truest point of their vocation.

Cardinal Joseph Bernardin is another example. After a period of turmoil in his life (sexual accusations later retracted), when he learned that he had pancreatic cancer, he seemed to walk headlong into the mystery of life and death. "In the final analysis, our participation in the paschal mystery—in the suffering, death, and resurrection of Jesus—brings a certain freedom: the freedom to let go, to surrender ourselves to the living God, to place ourselves completely in his hands. . . . The more we cling to ourselves and to others, the more we try to control our destiny—the more we lose the true sense of our lives, the more we are impacted by the futility of it all. It's precisely in letting go, in entering into complete union with the Lord, in letting him take over, that we discover our true selves."

In the months after September 11, we still find ourselves coping with three things:

- the catastrophic event (and what happened at the World Trade Center was catastrophic, no matter what caused it),
- a criminal act of terror aimed at all of us,
- and our own fears that a variation of these acts will be repeated in a different form on a timetable we cannot determine.

Each of these three conditions demands a payment from us in prolonged insecurity. The fear of terror is mentally debilitating; anticipated catastrophe is unnerving.

"Catastrophe" comes from the Greek, *kata*, "wrongly," and *strophe*, "turning." These sudden "wrong-turnings" in life become historical markers in the mind of the affected community. No matter when, no matter what. And the community always asks: Why?

We're quite aware that religion alone "cannot provide a solution to complex problems, but religion offers," as Marjorie Hope and James Young note, "guidance, a sense of boundaries, direction, and a responsive community." Religion, at its best, "represents the spirit animating all life."

After a deliberate act of terror, such as the destruction of the World Trade Center in Manhattan, and the attack on the Pentagon in Washington, and the death dive of the passenger jet into the Pennsylvania field, the wounds and scars inflicted by that original catastrophe are what the terrorist now continually aggravates. The haunting terrorist threat rekindles with acidic fear a burning apprehension. Li-Fu Tuan describes our dilemma: we want to prevent or circumvent a reoccurrence of the terror, but we barely know where to begin because we do not know its nature.

We only know our nature—to call for help and/or to flee.

Called upon in the smoke-filled stairways and fire-filled offices of the World Trade Center and the Pentagon on September 11, 2001, did God feel close? Or remote and more terrible? For the survivors and the families of the dead and injured, who or what now is God? God is the same Who, the same What. And in the same place as ever—wherever we are. Especially as we watch the aftermath unfold on television.

Monody in a Time of Disaster

The earth takes a deep breath.
The ground coughs,

a terrible thrust.
While in Chicago at 10 degrees
a Polish woman is kneeling
with her toes and bare feet
frozen to the floor.
Her last mile of sorrow
a broken pipe, a broken dream.
Do we mourn one death
or the thousands unknown?
Thoreau would not understand
the graphics of grieving
on a 27" screen.
—Kathleen Gunton

In our innocence and anxiety, in our humility, in our hesitation as to a way ahead, where and how do we begin to understand a God of suffering? A God who has generally been, for most of us, a God of kindness?

Dolores writes:

As a very structured personality, my tendency is to try to organize my world—to plan, to make lists, to see goals accomplished. I've been this way from as early as I can remember. As a young mother (four children in five years) life was "interruptions."

I kept looking for some way to understand this. I stumbled upon something Henri Nouwen had written about interruptions actually being the grace of the moment: the telephone, a crying child, an unexpected errand that needed doing. That helped.

Then big, really big interruptions occurred—my husband's cardiac events and declining health and all the accompanying fear, a pattern that has lasted well over two decades. These would be times when all the routines I cherish, mundane routines that I think give me security, are set aside. Instead, I spend time in the hospital or rehab clinic trying to hold my universe together.

In some deep place I know that I have no control over "interruptions," but still I keep on trying. Or is it that I am simply looking for a way to truly experience my dependence on God, ways to lean on the One who creates and sustains.

In Psalm 143, the speaker/singer pleads with God: "Let your good spirit guide me / in ways that are level and smooth. / For your name's sake, Lord, save my life" (Psalm 143:10–11).

I join with those I will never know but with whom I share God's world, and God's profound sorrow. I pray these lines with them.

At compline, the last prayer of the evening, I say this simple blessing: "May the all-powerful Lord grant us a restful night and a peaceful death." Indeed. A peaceful death seems a grace beyond all telling. I pray for all those in the darkness of New York and Washington and Pennsylvania.

I have searched out a cherished book, *An Interrupted Life: The Diaries of Etty Hillesum* (Henry Holt, New York, 1996).

Etty was a young, talented, secular Jewish woman living in Amsterdam during the Nazi occupation. Her world became smaller and smaller as more restrictions were placed on Jews. But her inner world became larger and larger. She found God, the God within, almost by accident. One entry reads: "If all this suffering does not help us to broaden our horizon, to attain a greater humanity by shedding all trifling and irrelevant issues, then it will all have been for nothing."

Etty's diaries are stunningly suitable. I shall return to them again and again. And like so many of us during this particular time, she will dine in a cafe, as if everything were normal.

Maybe it is.

2

Facing Fear with Faith

There is room for rational fear [of terrorism], because it is on the move.

—Archbishop Paul Hallinan

Faith is where we find the strength to relight the candles the hurricane of terrorism blew out.

Faith is not how we escape problems. When the world stares grimly at us, faith is how we look back. Faith gives us the ability to look the world in the eye.

There is reason to fear terrorism, but no reason to fear it blindly. The essence of fear burns us with the red-hot fires of September 11 that have seared our consciousness. What about the essence of faith? If fear is being terrified—at the mercy of whoever and whatever chooses to hurt us, burn us, kill us, exploit us—then faith links us to the other mercy—the merciful God.

Faith and hope are linked arm-in-arm. Philosophers and poets have labored on this link. Faith is the gift that requires work. Hope springs up, more an impulse, and requires a resolution. Faith is never resolved, but we don't need proof. We have accepted the gift.

What is it in faith that matters? What matters is our decision, our answer, when this question is posed: Are we convinced to the inner core of our being that through Christ Jesus' words and life God has touched us, touched us personally, and that we have responded to that touch of God? If we are convinced, then we know that we know God. However partially, and perhaps partly in our blindness, God is in our lives. With great fumbling and an embarrassing lack of articulation we believe so much we pray to God in faith. We believe in prayer as we believe in the tenets and testaments of our Christian tradition. We believe in and through the Gospels. "Credo." I believe. We hear God. We believe God. And we believe in God.

The fact is, though, we have to dwell on these things and go about our daily life and living. Not always knowing and not always having an answer—perhaps having only the suggestion of an answer.

Thich Nhat Hanh and a 3-Hole Punch

Thich Nhat Hanh and a 3-hole punch.
An egg for breakfast and soup for lunch.

Life is composed of books and things.
We read. We sew. The telephone rings.

Bones are broken and babies are born.
Laundry gets done in the early morn.

Children stray, then mend their lives.
God's aware and very wise.

We sleep. We wake. We do our tasks.
When life gets tough we wear our masks.

We meet the challenge day by day.
We change and grow along the way.

The bottom line . . . I have a hunch
Is Thich Nhat Hanh and a 3-hole punch.
—Marilyn Cunin

We don't always know where the faith came from. We only know it is there. And we accept it as a gift that is repeated in the Eucharist. And in the Word.

Some may want a rational explanation to belief but, being quite rational about it, belief doesn't add up to much in the cold light of terror on a beautiful day, does it?

We say we have a gift, but doubters say we can't show it to anyone. We can pass around books that contain the words of faith, but we can't prove the Son of Man actually said those words. Or that anyone who actually knew him wrote those words. They can watch us take a little bread and drink a little wine—they see that it's just a little piece of bread and they smell that it's just a bit of wine. We say this is the Body and Blood of Christ.

It doesn't seem like a very convincing show. Does it? Can you blame those who simply raise their eyebrows, sniff, and walk away?

So why do we believe? We believe because there is another element to the gift.

Faith / Life

One rose
Small, fluted, deep pink bud
Straining on its taut thorned stem
Into the vast empty air

One thrust
Of being, beauty, form
Challenging nothingness with life
Expiring into perfume

One life
A flash of energy
Tracing a single arc of truth
Against the bleak, dark void

One fierce bright yes
Indelible
Against the howling no
—Sandra M. Schneiders, I.H.M.

Mystery.

The mystery rests in that fact that something has been revealed to us, and we know it. People who do not believe, and will never believe, understand mystery even when they don't understand belief—not that we're always 100 percent certain. Archbishop Paul Hallinan said it well: "Even doubts can have two effects: although they can enervate and weaken faith, they can also try and test it. Catholics must not rest comfortably on their belief. We're called to suffer many a struggle of doubt." What the mystery impels us to do is what faith already says we must: "take up responsibility, to make the faith relevant to the community in which we live. To produce Christian witness rather than Christian bystanders."

Me?

Everything that lives
gives testimony.

Everything created
gives testimony.

But witness?
Witness is giving
testimony to/for

—everything created
—everything that lives.
—Alice Ward

Pope John XXIII wasn't just talking to bishops when he said we need to explore the mystery, "to probe into the mind of Christ."

Mystery may be simpler for us than we think. For we find that we share in it with others. The mystery is in what the Eucharist creates in us in communion with those around us. The mystery is in what the Word does to us when we take it into our own hearts and souls to ponder. Together or alone. It is the mystery that has us do in faith the best we can—as Christians. Pope Paul VI called mystery "a reality imbued with the presence of God."

Arthur writes:

When we are terrified we want God to hold our hand. What we desperately, self-lovingly, self-convincingly have to find is the strength and confidence that in this mystery God holds more than our hand. God holds our soul.

The Word tells us there is a price to pay for the gift of faith. So when I ask myself if I have faith, if I believe, I have to ask if I am prepared to pay the price of that belief.

I am fearful; I worry about being cowardly; I don't bear pain well.

In the abstract we can always say yes, but when concrete reality invades, what then?

Hidden Treasure

Make peace with pain.
Its coming, stealthy or sudden,
is certain as winter's sunset.
A chosen companion on our lifetime journey,
entrusted with blessed task to do.

Make friends with pain.
Embrace its searing scalpel touch
waiting to mine a cross of gold
buried deep within and waiting
your choice of fuller, richer life.
—Sister Maria Corona Crumback, I.H.M.

There are, I think, two forms of fear: fear you face and fear you live with. (Though I may be making distinctions that don't exist.) But this thought came to mind when my wife and I took our grandchildren, Tyler, six, and Sarah, four, to the park for a picnic. It was the Sunday following the attack on the World Trade Towers. The scene: blue sky, California sunshine, healthy kids in pretty play clothes, large family and neighborhood groups having barbecues, swings bobbing, and voices squealing. I thought of a time in the 1960s when we'd been to see the movie *On the Beach*.

In the movie there has been a nuclear explosion. As the deadly toxic cloud wafts slowly across the globe, the only people still alive are the Australians. The movie focuses on a picnic scene, on the people enjoying themselves before the disaster that they know is coming hits.

I still remember after almost forty years the nightmare I had the night after seeing the movie. In the nightmare there had been a nuclear explosion. I'd returned to the house to locate my own young children. By coincidence, Christine would have been about six and Michael about four at the time. In the dream, after the explosion, they were inside the house on tiny trampolines. They were bouncing slowly up and down, mindless and eyeless. Their eyes had melted in the glare. Alive, but dead, as in brain dead.

More than three decades later, in the California park,

> I looked at our grandchildren. They had found school friends and neighborhood kids to play with in the sandbox. And I thought there are some fears that don't go away. But even if they are ever present—and the nuclear threat and now terrorism are ever present—we do find a way to subdue the fears and continue.
>
> But those fears are never gone. We only subdue them.

The world is broken into fragments by narrow nationalistic ideals. The sole overarching mantle of quasi-uniformity at present is, unfortunately, solely economic: globalization. Unfortunately, the essential goal of globalization appears selfish—though all the First World nations deny they're putting their own needs first. The arguments in its defense seem woefully incomplete compared to the global peoples' needs. More reflection, more prayer about this serious matter is surely needed.

Scarred by the searing images of the September attack on America, numbed by the terrible death toll, horrified by the criminal brutality of those who caused it, we dare not forget that there was fear—and oppression and injustice—in the world before that day.

And there was fear in our lives. We tend to feel that fear in the past, even the recent past, differed in degree just because it differed in kind.

It didn't differ. Not even in the United States. We can ask that group of Americans, the generations alive and aware from 1945 on, who actually understood the capricious nature of life growing up "Under the Bomb." (And the word "capricious" is used deliberately. The writer, Iris Murdoch, contends that "accidents, not suffering, are our most authentic *memento mori*, memorial to death.) We move through life with intimations of doom, perhaps subliminally, but there nonetheless.

Intimation of Doom

There is a glitter of terror on the world,
The brightness of the leaves before a storm.
The sun of this weird day has run to cover.
Silence of wind gives deafening alarm.
Something more terrible than death goes over.

What is this wingedness of dark that dips
Out of Apocalypse?

Faces are lifted to a saffron sky.
What will rain down? The cowed earth holds its breath.
And each man knows what he would not repeat
In the last sound-proof cell of his retreat:
That good does not invariably triumph
This side of death.
—Jessica Powers

For forty years, and in fact still today, if one thinks about nuclear terrorism, the world has survived almost on a whim.

But we forgot about that.

For decades, the fingers on the constantly adjusted clock of the Bulletin of Atomic Scientists clicked closer to midnight. That meant that nuclear war, nuclear holocaust, was increasingly imminent.

In other moments, the clock's fingers moved counterclockwise away from midnight and the world breathed freer. With the meltdown of the Soviet Union, the world breathed more easily because one of the two contesting nuclear powers had disintegrated. Nuclear terrorism remained as a threat, but most people put it out of their minds.

Not any more.

No, the fact is, and September 11 has made it clear, that for the past two decades most of us have erred.

With the United States being the lone superpower, we, its beneficiaries, have built up a vision of what life is and was, and was intended to be. We built this vision on the quite meager evidence of our own hopes and experiences of very recent times.

We didn't even factor in our parents' or grandparents' experiences, thinking that because they had gone before there could not be any parallels to match their generation's anxieties, deprivations, or war-torn-world-ness.

All of this tells us paradoxically that the Americans possibly best equipped to handle fear, the fear evident in the post-September terrorist-inspired uncertainties of life, may be those Americans who have already experienced and lived through that life-threatening uncertainty. We can learn from the stoicism—and optimism—of the younger ones who risk their lives to arrive here illegally to find a better life. They know the stories of many others in Mexico, for example, who have perished en route at the hands of those who prey on migrants as robber bands once preyed on pilgrims.

These human beings know they might perish in the waterless wide spaces just across the border, where the sun kills those caught unprepared for the trek ahead. These are the least among us, the newly arrived. They come with nothing. Christianity makes us look at things back to front, opposite the way society views things. Otherwise, why would we think there were survival lessons to be learned from the examples of the poor, the weak, and the sick? But who displays more courage than the person with a crushing mental illness who, haunted daily, nonetheless finds ways to get through that day, the person who deals with more uncertainty even than those with terminal illnesses?

Seen this way, it isn't surprising that, faced with an irrational terrorism, those who personify the refusal to give up, to not despair, may be the very elderly Americans who, now in their late eighties, graduated from high school in 1929. They saw the America that had offered promise all through their school years collapse into the chaos of the Depression, into national hunger and joblessness, into hopelessness and helplessness. They had no sense and no real promise that things would get better for them. There are still those among us who remember the rag pickers of the 1930s, forerunners perhaps of today's homeless.

The Rag Man

The rag man's cry has summits like a song.
Far down the street I hear his music stir:
The shrill unhurried wheels that would prolong
An endless journey, the slow clomp of hoofs,
The cry with spires, with little pointed roofs.
I think of what Teresa said to Jesus,
And how He answered her:

"I go where no one else would dare to venture.
I gather what the angels would not touch."
O Jew, is the heart's cloth then worth so much
That its soiled scraps would drive Thee to this buying,

This walking through the streets, this endless crying,
Leading Thy donkey through the fetid slums
Down streets no other rag man ever knew,
Waiting at doors until a sharp voice comes,
"Down from my doorstep, Jew."

Jesus, when thou hast reached this alleyway,
Stop at the broken door and presently
One will come forth to deal this day with Thee,
One who computes the value of her love
By Thy dignity.
—Jessica Powers

Some might retort that our nightmare, the September 11 terrorist attack, is different, that "it isn't the same!"

The answer is, it's never the same twice.

As Mark Twain said, history doesn't repeat itself, but it sure does rhyme. Twain meant that events can be similar enough to what went before that we can sometimes take lessons from the past. These Americans are our lessons, from the past and the present.

To end uncertainty, we want peace. We don't want to join in that macabre dance of Death, the "circle of violence." We don't want other people's children and families killed in searching for that peace. We want guidance for our behavior, even our thoughts, as we grapple with what living with death has come to mean, in a new way since September 11, 2001.

Faith isn't an only child. It has a twin, endurance. Faith and endurance have a duty, the duty that is constant from having made the commitment. In combination, these words state—and the German language emphasizes it best: *Ich Dienst*—"I must." I must because I have said to Jesus, "I will." "I must" is what I say to myself. And I find faith and endurance in the commitment.

Dolores writes:

John Lahr, writing in *The New Yorker,* said "catastrophe has imposed on America a profound, unmooring sense of the unknown, and at this particular time we have to protect not just our external world but our internal one. This requires vigilance, an insistence on living with ambiguity, on thinking against received opinion, and mastering anxiety."

September 11 was almost like an invasion from another world. And one can't help but notice that visitations from other worlds engender fear.

Over and over when angels enter into the world of humankind they caution us to "fear not."

The caution is against the paralyzing fear that drains our ability to act. The angelic greeting also recognizes that sensible people do, indeed, experience fear in the face of "otherness." We should not confuse that fear with a lack of courage. "That" fear, fear of the Lord (which the Hebrew Scriptures tell us is the beginning of wisdom), is more akin to awe.

Think of Aslan (the first Lion king) in C. S. Lewis's allegory, *The Lion, The Witch and the Wardrobe: A Story for Children* (Collier, New York, 1970, pp. 75–76). The children in the tale are being told of the expected return of the true king, Aslan, and they inquire if he is safe. "Safe?" responds the Beaver who told the children about the king. "Who said anything about safe? 'Course he isn't safe. But he's good. He's the King, I tell you."

In fact, the Beaver has it just right. God cannot be domesticated, brought down to size, made to conform to our often self-serving wills, but this does not mean God is not love; it's just not the Hallmark version. I do not imply that God is not to be found in the details of our domestic lives, our intimate love, and our everyday generosity.

We set a table to share our food; this is an act of courtesy which conveys respect. Repeated over and over again such small acts ready us for acts of courtesy and respect when something unexpected occurs: a friend falls seriously ill; a neighbor is called up in the Army reserves; a son or daughter announces their conscientious objection to war.

Such an announcement can strike fear in one's heart—what will family and neighbors think? So it helps to remember the angelic counsel, "Fear not!" but it is also important to ponder that annunciations, profound encounters, change forever the pattern of life. Critic George Steiner in *Real Presences* (University of Chicago Press, 1989, p. 143), calls such an annunciation "a terrible beauty," or gravity breaking into the small house of our cautionary being. This small house of ours is no longer habitable in the same way. So it was with Mary of Nazareth, and so it has ever been.

Novelist, poet, and essayist Reynolds Price, in a moving memoir titled *A Whole New Life* (Atheneum, New York, 1994, p.183), vividly illustrates what transformation really is. In 1984 he experienced what he calls "a mid-life collision with cancer and paralysis." It was cancer of the spine, inoperable, treatable only with radiation. His story is one of unexpected incursions from other worlds, an unanticipated encounter with Christ, and an auditory experience of God. For a non-churchgoer these encounters were mystifying, but as real as anything he had known.

The physical finale of his battle with cancer is his permanent confinement to a wheelchair. The emotional, spiritual, artistic finale has not yet happened. Since the cancer, Price's creativity seems to have been turned loose. He says of himself that while he was always watchful (such are the ways of writers) he is now even more so: he can't escape from others, from situations.

He observes, watches, learns. His literary output has been astonishing. He also has advice for those whose life is turned upside down by tragedy (by annunciations?): "Grieve for a decent limited time over whatever parts of your old self you know you'll miss. Next, find your way to be somebody else, the next viable you." His point is that the old self is gone, and you must help the new self emerge.

And he cautions, "Your mate, your children, your friends at work—anyone who knew or loved you in your old life—will be hard at work in the fierce endeavor to revive your old self, the self they recall with love and respect."

This is all to the good, he says. It proves that you're loved and valued and wanted, but you must continue on the search for the new or deeper self. "If you don't discover that next appropriate incarnation of who you must be, and then become that person at a stiff trot, you'll be no good whatever again to the ruins of your old self, not to any friend or mate who's standing beside you in hopes of a hint that you're feeling better this instant and are glad of company."

There is wisdom here not only for those personally traumatized by the September events and the ones that followed, but also for communities and perhaps for the nation. We say, "Nothing will be the same," but what does this mean? It can mean that we are in the process of conversion, an exciting prospect for people of faith, but a frightening one, too.

The old self (individual and corporate) is so familiar, and we want to cling. And I know about clinging, about resistance to change. It often takes an intervention, an annunciation, to release my grasp on what has been.

One of the great blessings of age is memory. Memory helps assuage the debilitating effects of fear. Memory reminds me of my own long history of God's mercy. Yes, I still fear death (or at least dying); I still fear the unknown. But then I pause, and I remember that glimpses into the unknown have brought a certain kind of peace, and that over and over again I have tasted mercy.

Carmelite poet Jessica Powers (*The Selected Poetry of Jessica Powers,* ed. Regina Siegfried, A.S.C., and Robert F. Morneau, ICS Publications, Washington, DC, 1999) writes in "The Mercy of God":

> *I am copying down in a book from my heart's archives*
> *the day that I ceased to fear God with a shadowy fear.*

She goes on to speak of the journey to truthfulness about who she is and who God is.

I walked out of myself and went into the woods
of God's mercy,
and here I abide.

The poem moves into a song of union and it concludes with these lines:

And I fear God no more; I go forward to wander forever
in a wilderness made of His infinite mercy alone.

Is this not the time to enumerate God's infinite mercies?

Job, above all, must have wondered about God's mercies. That suffering prophet certainly learned the lesson of God as reality.

Job endures loss over and over again until it seems that nothing, absolutely nothing is left. But of course there is something left: his belief in God, and his belief in his own integrity. "Though he kill me, yet I will trust in him" (Job 13:15).

When at last God answers Job's complaints, there is divine confirmation that suffering is not always deserved. And God goes on to give a sweeping description of reality, the terrors of living on earth.

Job's reply to the Lord is notable for its direct simplicity. "I know that you can do all things, and that no purpose of yours can be thwarted. . . . Therefore I have uttered what I did not understand, things too wonderful for me, which I did not know. . . . I had heard of you by the hearing of the ear, but now my eye sees you; therefore I despise myself, and repent in dust and ashes" (Job 42:2–6).

Where was God when Job was being stripped of every self-image he had cherished, every person he had loved, every understanding he had clung to about God? God was with him.

We have our motivation: to get on with life. Yet the daily confrontation with the taunting fear of terrorism tells us that we may need better spiritual armor than what we've clothed ourselves with to date. In examining what we think of as faith, we need to be in a gardening mood, ready to sink our fingers down into the soil of our personal thought patterns. The bulbs, corms, and rhysomes of our already-blossomed thought patterns ought, like the gardener's originals in the fall, to be dug up and trimmed, split and transplanted. Family, community, beauty, prayer, and contemplation will help us do it.

We have to embrace life with our new philosophy, our fresh spirituality—life to be lived. Life to be lived by the minute and the hour and the day. The life abundant, abundant simply because we are in it to embrace it. By embracing others.

The human tendencies at times of the most fearsome stress are to want to hide, or to want to do something. The want to "do" something is fine. Action based on prayer and reflection, and not just "gut reaction," means that in all likelihood we're doing something correct or useful. Yet again, when the world suddenly changes, as everyday life in the United States has changed following that dreadful slaughter, even the believer doesn't always know what to reflect on, or how to pray, or what to say to God—or what to do. Perhaps the best action is inaction, meaning not starting something solely in order to be doing something. Thought must come first.

There's a story told from Australia from before World War II, probably apocryphal. An Australian farmer, sensitive to world events, foresaw the likelihood of war with Japan. Australians feared that overcrowded Japan was eyeing nigh-empty Australia (much as the Australians fear Indonesia is doing today). Not wanting to subject his family to that risk, the farmer bought a plantation on a Pacific island and moved. The island was called Guadalcanal. It was the scene of some of the bloodiest fighting in the war in the Pacific.

Fear provokes questions such as these: Will things get better than this? How? What's coming next? Can we cope? At what price peace?

We can cope, and we can adjust. Even if there are new outrages, we shall find within us the means of taking the uncertain, the unpredictable, the violent, the unimaginable into account. We do it all the time. In a simple way, driving ten miles an hour above the speed limit among the trucks doing seventy, we're doing it. Every time we embark on a transatlantic or transpacific flight, we do it.

Flying in America

We wait silently in snaking lines,
slouching towards security.
No companionable murmurs or impatient sighing,
just the repeating drone of low-paid workers
    searching for the next
apocalypse.
"Bring out your laptops," they chant.
We shuffle, juggle, obey.

The airport newsstands, united.

Front covers immortalizing new icons of death.
Passengers are but moments away
    from mentally reenacting the
unimaginable.
Why buy images already boxcut into our souls?

We rewrite and rewrite cartoon scripts on takeoff.
ACTION!
She grabbed the pots of scalding coffee from the tiny
    galley and
aimed real low.
SPLASH! WHAMO! ARRGH!
The bad guy instantly felled by Starbucks!

The universe was saved!
and . . . CUT!

In flight, I glance at the magazine my subconscious
willed me to buy.
Ridiculously perfect papier-mâché pumpkins
grace the cover.
Good god! It's Martha Stewart's
LIVING.

The secret of forcing spring blooming daffodils to
flower indoors, in winter,
is revealed.
Their names roll off my tongue.
Golden Harvest.
Bridal Crown.
JetFire,
Pink Angel.
Imagine.
Imagine all the daffodils living life in peace.

Flight attendants are sniffling into shredded tissue.
2,700 of their coworkers were laid off yesterday. Their
jobs may be
gone
when we land.
The single cell of Martha Stewart in me would like
desperately to make it all
beautiful.
"You're doing a good job," I say.
"America's gonna keep flying."
But what I really want to do
is grab the microphone and shout,
"Attention ladies and gentlemen,

we are about to learn how to keep on LIVING.
And today we're going to learn how to bloom
in the dead
of our winter."
—C. Richardson

We trust our lives to intricate machinery that is fallible, to an aircraft that is heavier than air and heavier than the water it would very rapidly sink into. We play life's odds at every minute. We're constantly at risk. Witness the slab of metal that dropped off the Bay Bridge and killed a motorist underneath. The passengers in the train, safely sleeping, when the barge hits the bridge. The drive-by shootings.

We hear these stories; we share the pain; we shake our head in wonderment—and we find the faith to go on.

Dolores lives about two miles from the perimeter of the Pentagon. Some of her children and grandchildren live in the immediate area. Dolores knows that for all time the region in which she lives—a strategic area immediately abutting the nation's capital—is a "Ground Zero" in the minds of terrorists. Death, she finds, has taken on new dimensions even though that's where she works and does her chores on a daily basis (she's a fellow at the Woodstock Theological Center). From time to time, she walks across the street from her apartment to spend time with the elderly and sick in an independent living community. She spends time with folks who live with impending death in a traditional way. Intermittently, as a retreat leader, she will continue to travel. This, too, is facing fear with faith.

Dolores writes:

When the towers crumbled and the Pentagon crash shook the small cottage in which my daughter lives, I kept on with routines: household chores, work commitments, the structures and routines that give form to my life.

The Catholic Church's "Morning Prayer" and "Compline" (the last prayer service of the day) are part of this structure. The Compline psalm for Tuesday night September 11 was Psalm 143, "prayer in distress." The lines seemed especially appropriate for this dreadful day:

The enemy pursues my soul;
he has crushed my life to the ground;
he has made me dwell in darkness
like the dead, long forgotten.
Therefore my spirit fails;
my heart is numb within me.

These words are for those under concrete and steel, windowless, lampless. There's more:

I remember the days that are past:
I ponder all your works.
I muse on what your hand has wrought
and to you I stretch out my hands.
Like a parched land my soul thirsts for you.

Arthur writes:
Fear raises the specter of a fiercesome God. Some use, indeed prefer, the idea of a fierce, smiting, and rough-justice God as bedrock belief. They want a God who threatens, cajoles, and cows people into obedience. This is not the God of this journey.

Nor is the God of this journey the kindly, munificent friend. There is a strong tendency in the United States, for Christians living amidst great abundance, or, like most of us, with a high degree of personal comfort, to see God as a source of things for this life.

The German actor Hildegard Knef lived for more than a decade in southern California in the 1950s and 1960s. She made movies in the United States before returning permanently to Germany decades ago. Knef grew up in Berlin during the Allied bombing of World War II. Night after night, squadrons of planes carrying thousands of tons of explosives dropped them relentlessly on one German city after another; and German children sought protection in the deep, cold cellars of homes, churches, and schools.

Twenty-five years later, Knef writes about the distinctions in how God looks in such totally different settings as peacetime prosperous California and wartime Germany. The southern Californians grouped around the Hollywood film colony she described as "warmhearted and successful, handsome and relaxed. Happy children enjoying happy marriages and happy babies. Many of them mention God, who has been good to them and answered their prayers, sending them the husband, the wife, the undeserved success."

To these Americans, writes Knef, "HE becomes a gigantic ear hovering in the heavens over the West Coast, ever alert, ever ready to accept and deliver new orders for success if addressed in the proper manner" (*The Gift Horse: Report on a Life,* Dell Publishing, New York, 1972, p. 176).

Here in America, she says, God "is tangible and generous, a champion." She recalled that in wartime Berlin, the God "called upon in heaving cellars had seemed remoter. And more terrible."

When I was a child, throughout May 1940, it was the Germans who night after night dropped bombs on the street where I lived.

The aircraft used the burning houses on sloping North Road as an approach light to their targets, the Cammell Lairds shipyards that lay beyond, on the south bank of the River

Mersey, and the huge harbor and docks that were Liverpool, on the north bank. The old Victorian house we lived in was large enough to have two kitchens. In one was constructed a steel air raid shelter with double bunk beds. Night after night we three kids and my mother huddled in there—my father was always up at the hospital. We listened for the bombs. We heard them coming. Then we felt the ground and the house shaking. Soon we were coughing from decades of soot and dust shaken loose from a half-dozen chimneys. Or my mother and elder brother were dashing from the shelter momentarily to replace the boards blown out of the glassless windows.

We clung to prayer. We lived in childish hope on the basis of a simple utterance. The prayer was:

> *Our Lady of Mount Carmel,*
> *Watch over us and pray for us this long night through,*
> *And keep us safe*
> *From all harm and danger.*

Mount Carmel is a towering headland facing the Mediterranean, part of the mountain range that stretches southeastward from Haifa, Israel. Karmel is an orchard, a pleasant woodland, with a reputation as a holy place for more than three thousand years. In Arabic it is *Jebel Mar Elyas,* the Mountain of the Lord Elia.

In the Catholic tradition, this prayer dates back at least a thousand years in some form. The Christian hermits later known as the Carmelites lived here in their little beehive monasteries. And they blended their meditative way of life as communal and personal solitude, praying to God, modeling Jesus, with a devotion also to his mother, Mary.

The images conjured up by the one prayer depend on the moment. The images range from a sense of sanctuary to thoughts of a pleasant woodland, from the continuity of life across thousands of years to the comfort and reassurance to be found in meditation.

God and prayer can provide insights into life and continuity and do begin to meet our need for solace, for a comforting, for someone to keep us safe from all harm and danger.

We crave reassurance, but we have to be careful from whom we take it, and in what form we accept that reassurance. There is no escape into material things, no matter how temporarily comforting. Rich and poor alike died September 11. There is blessed refuge in loving arms but not, finally, protection. September 11 tells us, as does every catastrophe, that life is lived surrounded by harm and danger. We're seeking in faith, prayer, contemplation and Christian action the strength to joyfully live life fully despite the risks. The only reassurance we really have is from the God who said, "Fear not" (John 12:15).

No, I'll amend that.

Our assurances come from God and from the very fact that God has kept us alive with yet a little more time—and the mind to face and shape the future—conscious decision time.

Dolores writes:

A nearby mosque held an open house on the Saturday almost three weeks after the catastrophic events of September. My husband and I attended. This is a community grounded in faith, hospitality, optimism, and confidence in the teachings of their religious tradition. There were study sessions: short lectures and questions. In my "section," lots of questions. A Jewish man had read the first hundred pages of the Qur'an and saw in it a strong condemnation of Jews and Christians.

The lecturing imam answered in terms of history and culture. He said that the Holy Book was written (revealed) over a period of twenty-three years and that in the early period there were conflicts between followers of the Prophet and certain groups of Jews and Christians. He cautioned everyone to read on—the message of peace is further on, he said.

The open house was more than lectures on Islam. There was food (lots of it—served by men!) and informal conversations between Western visitors and members of the mosque in various versions of appropriate simple, modest dress. The atmosphere was one of peace and welcome.

The meaning of Islam was explained over and over—linguistically, it means surrender, submission to God, a concept not foreign to Christians.

Perhaps this is a time of strange blessing, a time when we discover how interwoven our lives really are with strangers.

A few days after September 11, a family member who works in lower Manhattan went in search of a copy of the Qur'an. The Greenwich Village bookshop he frequents was sold out of the sacred text. Instead, the shopkeeper handed him a copy of Karen Armstrong's *History of God* (Ballantine Books, New York, 1994), and now John is immersed in the intertwining stories of Judaism, Christianity, and Islam. This comes as a blessing to John, whose wife is Jewish and whose daughter was recently engaged to a Muslim. He is trying to make sense of a world he never envisioned during his Catholic school days, and the Greenwich Village shopkeeper has helped.

Who knows what strange adventures in grace await us, no matter how meager our faith. A grain of mustard seed is enough for the moment, so says our Lord.

3

Facing Fear with Hope

A real renewal cannot come out of a vacuum. Renewal is formed by present needs and fresh insights. It must draw its strength chiefly from the God-guaranteed treasures of the centuries since he said, "I will be with you all days."

—Archbishop Paul Hallinan

Hope is the springboard to renewal. When we hope, we hope for a change in some present circumstance. The greatest hope is that, compelled as Christians by what happened on September 11 to bring solace, change, and assurance, we are engaged on a particular journey. It is a pilgrimage to the place where we "fix," where we "anchor," the role of the Church in twenty-first-century American society. We get there by showing that from our two thousand years of teaching and tradition, this church, at this time, has something specific to say to the country and to the world.

The Second Vatican Council (1962–65) issued a document called *Gaudium et spes*—literally, "Joy and Hope." We'll reflect on some of its words shortly.

Hope is an impulse, a swelling up of something. Hope genuinely is a form of happiness (sometimes short-lived and therefore something easily dashed). The happiness in hope comes from anticipation of good, or better, awaiting us.

Christian hope doesn't travel alone.

Christian hope is always pulling a little red wagon called patience. They never go anywhere the one without the other. Two allied attributes hitch a ride in the wagon. The one hitchhiker is beauty, a way of sustaining the hope. The other is vocation. The decision over one's Christian vocation in life is made in anticipation. One responds to the call, the *vocation*, in hope.

Patience, first. Then beauty. And on to vocation.

Patience

She waited, she waited, she waited, she did.
He hesitated, hesitated, hesitated and hid.

He longed, and he longed and he longed and he sighed.
I'm wronged, she said, wronged, said she, wronged
and he lied.

But he hadn't, he hadn't, he hadn't, was scared.
So in courage, in courage, in courage, she dared

Sought and found him, she found him she did,
And they made their wee home in the place where he hid.

But opened and opened and opened its door
So her hope, love and courage had the world to explore.
—John Sladen Whittle

In the story of this pair (above), one of them had to have hope and the courage to act. Love alone wasn't enough. They needed her hope so they could use the love and courage to explore.

Arthur writes:

Jesus and the Catholic living tradition talk often about the need to be like little children. It can be a bit tedious because we don't always know how to apply it. But I was in the park the other day, paused on my bike as three little kids in the six to seven year age range, talked about getting home. They seemed to be neighbors rather than siblings.

One boy had a bike, one a scooter, and the little girl had neither. In a charitable gesture that was also two parts hope and one part faith, the boy with the bike said, "I'll scoot forward on my seat. You climb on and *hold on to me.* I've never done this before."

And this is what Jesus wants of us. Our hope and our energies in the attempt to pull it off as we encourage others: "Hold on to me. I've never done this before."

The call to vocation, the beckoning of natural beauty, and the beauty created by human hands, all contain anticipation. Beauty has within it a commanding or a gentle beckoning.

Beauty in all its forms starts in someone (for what is beauty resides in the eyes of the beholder) a slow-moving or quick-paced kaleidoscope of patterns of what might be. It reaches in beyond the first level of emotions and sounds its chords on the diaphragm of the soul. The music is hope's main attraction: promise. Hence, the happiness.

Christian hope is more than a dream imagined when one is awake. It is more like what the English poet George Herbert (d. 1633) was hinting at in *Outlandish Proverbs* when he called hope "a dance." When the dancer stops, "the dance" disappears. English composer Sydney Carter, who created "The Lord of the Dance" to an old Shaker melody, was offering the Lord as the hope and the dance as the way: "I am the Lord of the Dance, said he."

"I am the Lord of hope, dancing into the future," he might have said.

We hope that terrorism and fear will go away. If this is not a vain hope we at least already know it is a distant hope. So we hope we can deal with the terrorism and fear that won't go away. And this is not a vain hope. Theologian Richard P. McBrien, in talking of hope as a power (a virtue: *virtus*; power), places hope midway between "presumption" and "despair."

"Presumption" presumes all will turn out as precisely as we wish (which surely summons up the warning, be careful what you wish for). "Despair" presumes there will be no change or improvement at all. McBrien, in a sense, also sees hope dancing ahead of us when he writes: "Hope is oriented to the Kingdom of God, not as heaven alone, but as renewal and re-creation of the whole world. God is not above us but ahead of us, summoning us to co-create the future" (*Catholicism*, Winston Press, Minneapolis, MN, 1966, p. 973). Summoning us to join the dance.

McBrien shows Christian hope as anticipatory knowledge based in faith. Anticipation that somehow, even in these dreadful times, we can as Christians, individually and in community, co-create a better future. To do this, hope has to have the patience necessary to solidly team up with the endurance that is faith. Beauty helps with the patience, because beauty alters the time frame. We can see beauty daily even when we can't find hope daily.

Dolores writes:

Hope is creative and energizing. When we hope for something we strive to come up with ideas that will bring the hope to fruition. But hope has to be sustained. As Proverbs 13:12 cautions us, "Hope deferred makes the heart sick."

I believe that finding beauty in daily life is the single, strongest sustaining force that hope can draw on. With beauty around us as a sign of promise, "hope" doesn't shrivel into bitterness. Some years ago I was living and studying in the West Bank, two miles from Jerusalem and an equal distance from Bethlehem. Each day we witnessed Israeli soldiers detaining Palestinians and each day militant Palestinians deepened the sense of threat and fear.

Strangely, the tension of this difficult situation was matched with the intensity of that land's beauty. The ancient architecture, the hard desert where a drop of water called forth varieties of wild flowers, the afternoon light that lingered on the hills until every rock glowed—all this nurtured hope as we prayed for the peace of the land we called holy.

Can I dare to hope that terrorism will one day be laid aside? Can I dare to hope that one day all the world's slaughter will end? I can dare. This is the essence of Christian hope. In the mid-nineteenth century in the United States there were those who hoped and dared and worked that slavery would be over. These hopes are not always realized in our own lifetimes. Many of those who worked to free others from bondage never lived to see the day. But their hopes lived on and fed into that final result.

Beauty is one aspect of the hope contained within ordinary, everyday life.

Thirty years ago I read a story about a sister who left classroom teaching to work in a public housing project in Chicago. She helped the women there to arrange their space in such a way as to highlight the beauty already present (although hidden), or to create a spot of beauty at little or no cost.

Uncluttering the space, placing a wooden chair by the window to catch the sunlight, a bare table holding an arrangement of weeds collected along the railroad tracks—every bit as lovely as an English country garden.

Bare hallways became murals, as the sister and the women worked together. I've remembered this story all these years because the women had been helped to see in new ways. (As the story helped me to see in new ways, too.) And I hoped that the women's attention to beauty (and mine) would move into ever wider circles because beauty, like love (and other things of God), is diffusive of itself.

My first glimpse of London was filled with wonder, not because of Buckingham Palace or Big Ben or Picadilly. I was filled with wonder at the abundance of flowers growing out of the remaining rubble of wartime. The Blitz was over, and what was left was beautiful. A walk through the city would reveal a pile of stone (and who knows what else) that seemed to be nurturing primroses and other brilliant flora. To me, London was a city of surprising beauty. When I mentioned this to English colleagues at Stratford, they replied that Londoners themselves had turned to one of their distinctive activities—gardening—to revive hope.

Later that summer, I walked the moors of northern England and spent time in the Welsh countryside, but neither the ambiance of these places, nor the tranquility of the Avon River looked quite as beautiful as the floral transformation wrought by the Londoners.

New York City in the year 2001 has stirred this memory of long ago. I've heard one suggestion that a multitude of trees of all different kinds should be planted where the towers of steel and glass once stood, a living memorial to those who died there. The suggestion reminds me of something attributed to Martin Luther, who allegedly said that if he thought the world would end the next day, he would plant a tree.

In these days of grief and war I continue to read Etty Hillesum *(An Interrupted Life)* and her response to the impending doom of the Dutch Jewish community during World War II. I see how the theme of honoring one's ordinary duties reveals an inherent beauty and stokes the flame of hope.

At one point Etty begins to feel an indestructible resilience, not in a material sense, but in some deeper, spiritual way. "[T]he main thing is that even as we die a terrible death we are able to feel right up to the very last moment that life has meaning and beauty, that we have realized our potential and lived a good life."

Perhaps our roots will grow ever deeper and stronger during these days and months and maybe years of uncertainty and fear, as we realize that what exists is NOW, and it is pregnant with possibilities. What is needed is a lens to see the sacred in the ordinary. The practice of attentiveness can help construct such a lens. Can I concentrate on this single winter flower sheltered in a stone wall? Will I be totally present to the salad I'm trying to construct?

Evelyn Underhill (d. 1941), an astute Anglican English laywoman who wrote prolifically on the mystical life, says that through concentrating on the particulars we can enter into communion with the universal. It's surely worth trying.

Several years ago, before September 11, before the bombs fell in Afghanistan, before so many inventive twists on war appeared, I read an account of life in Kabul shortly after the Taliban takeover.

Winter had come, and it was particularly severe. Afghans spent their time waiting in line for bread distributed by the United Nations, the main sustenance for families without money, without work, without warmth. Firewood and bread were all that mattered that winter. The article concluded with a description of the bakeries where the relief bread was actually made. Women worked all day in severe heat, inhaling soot, their hands aching from their labors. My first reaction was to feel sorry for them.

But they told the reporter that they were happy. They at least had work, and they had bread at the end of the day to feed their families. And for a number of hours each day, they were warm. In an earlier time, before the Taliban, many of these women were nurses or teachers, with a life not unlike mine. And then, everything changed. Except their capacity to tap into the source of happiness and hope. Reading their story, I felt that Christ must surely be in the bread they baked and broke and shared. They probably would not name the sacred reality "Christ."

No matter. Their story, their life evoked gratitude in me. And hope.

I've wondered about these women since the United Nations has had to close the bakeries. Remembering them and the hope that will not die enlarges my small world and nourishes my soul. I pray for them in thanksgiving, remembering some lines from Jessica Powers's poem, "If You Have Nothing":

> *If you have nothing, gather back your sigh,*
> *and with your hands held high, your heart held high,*
> *lift up your emptiness.*

Arthur writes:

We came from hope and were born into hope. Hope is new life. And there are two types of new life: the newborn and the reborn. Nothing matches that moment when a newborn infant, for the first time, wraps his or her tiny hand around one's little finger. The connection is made. For us, here, to make that connection, all we need is a lullaby.

The Latch-String to Happiness

> *Good night, little baby—*
> *I've counted your toes*
> *I've kissed all your fingers,*
> *And rumpled your nose.*

Good night, little baby—
The day's gone away,
The big tired darkness
Doesn't know how to pray.

Good night, little baby—
My arms are the bed,
My heart is the pillow,
My love is the spread.
—Nina Isabel Jennings

This is only a lullaby, but offering it immediately presents us with two challenges.

The first has to do with its sentimentality. This lullaby reflects its 1909 origins. Is it too cloying? One can understand what provokes the question. Yet the answer is no; the lullaby is not at all cloying—if the mother or grandmother singing it knows the baby's father died in a stairwell in a World Trade Center building. Not too sweet if the parent singing it is anxious about bringing a child into this world. Not inappropriate if the baby is at risk, as we all are, from an attacker who can strike anywhere, with anything. And it's just a plain and lovely lullaby if the person singing it simply loves the child and the moment. Insincerity is what dilutes genuine sentiment into the mush of sentimentality.

The second challenge is the hope. Everything we believe in we try to will to that infant whose finger is wrapped around ours. Or whose head in the blanket has eyes closed in the perfect trust that our shoulder or our arms are sanctuary.

There is something to this connection to the miracle of life, of new birth, that broadcasts hope and reinforces the joy of simply being alive. And who is more alive than the children? The children around us, whether ours or not, provide hope. They provide us with a responsibility for the children, and to them—to teach them responsibility, too.

There's hope in the other Infant.

The Infant's Eyes

The light from his face was nothing
To cause one to cover the eyes,
To stand back in awe,
To stir the silent, secret places of the heart.

His was only a tiny infant face,
Smudged with dust here and there,
With small lips that quivered from the cold
And framed by straw entangled hair.

Yet, something in the eyes
Told of worlds where light never fades,
Where warm winds blow
And tears never fall.

It was the eyes
That made the heart beat faster,
That held the mind spellbound,
That awakened dreams of eternal days,
Life unending,
Love forever everywhere.
—Father Augustine John Moore

Augustine Moore writes of the light of the Infant's eyes. The following text on light is an excerpt from composer Mortern Lauridsen's "Lux Aeterna":

O light most blessed, fill the innermost heart
of all your faithful. . . .

Cleanse what is sordid, moisten what is arid,
heal what is hurt.
Flex what is rigid, fire what is frigid,
correct what goes astray. . . .

"Correct what goes astray." We're astray. We need the correction that comes when we absorb and live the joy and hope that has little to do with superficial optimism.

What are those superficial optimisms that, as insincerity dilutes sentiment, dilute genuine hope into its parodies? Naïve optimism is Voltaire's Dr. Pangloss: "All is for the best in the best of all possible worlds." It is Pollyanna, the persistently optimistic girl heroine in Eleanor H. Porter's nineteenth-century books. Pollyanna gave us a new word for our lexicon, and did us a disservice. She may have felt every cloud has a silver lining though, in fact, some clouds contain nothing but the storm to come. Terrorism can strike like lightning can strike.

To find the hope needed in the face of that storm requires that we reach very deeply into ourselves, and into our faith tradition. (And reach out to each other in community.) Not everyone telling us what God expects from our hopes has it right. More likely it comes down to what in the viscera of our soul the gathered momentum tells us is correct to hope for.

Our hope has muscle to it, authority even. Robert McClory captures this play between hope that gives up and hope that doesn't quit—and the authority of God-given visceral hope—as he writes about the impact on him of the play *The Miracle Worker* in *Faithful Dissenters: Stories of Men and Women Who Loved and Changed the Church* (Orbis, Maryknoll, NY, 2000).

There's a moment in the play, McClory says, that had a profound effect on him. Not the dramatic conclusion, "the great climax when [Helen Keller's] trapped mind is liberated." Rather, it is the moment when Annie Sullivan defines hope. Explains McClory: "For months, Annie has been attempting to break through, to open the girl's mind, but without success. Helen remains willful and wild, and the Keller family is prepared to give up hope, to place her in an institution for the mentally retarded. Sullivan pleads for more time in which to impart to Helen's 'new eyes' through the touch alphabet. Speaking from his own experience, the wisdom of age, and his acceptance of limitation, Helen's father says, 'Perhaps God may not have meant Helen to have the eyes you speak of.' And Annie retorts, '*I* mean her to!' "

Asks McClory, in a question that is its own answer: "Where was God at this moment? In the wisdom and experience of the father, or in the arrogant determination of Sullivan?"

Sometimes we just have to do it, keep going. Not blindly. Purposefully. This is the prophet of the Hebrew Scriptures in all of us who possess passion and compassion. But Jesus didn't leave us there. The ancient prophet he reinforced by a faith as current as the present moment, with a driving, forceful hope demanding change—from us. Demanding change from the world. Whether the world attends to our hopes for it is immaterial to the Christian. The demand is that the faith-driven hope be turned into action. Success is not in the Christian equation. And others may speak ill of us for daring to hope—in a progress outside the secular world's ability to comprehend.

Arthur writes:

The first New Testament I ever received as a young man, and still have, is an 1820 edition of the 1582 Douay (Douai) Testament. Pius VII, writing in that year in the frontispiece, tells the vicars apostolic (Britain had no Catholic bishops at that point): "Direct all your zeal and attention to this, that all the faithful, whom we have committed to your pastoral care,

> love one another in Charity, Sincerity, and Truth; that in the present general agitation, they shew themselves an example of good works; that they obey the King, and be so dutiful and faithful to him that our adversaries may fear (not having it in their power) to speak ill of us."
>
> Here in the United States, with the protections of a religious freedom not present in early nineteenth-century Britain, the reverse is the case. It is our obligation to not worry about whether "our adversaries speak ill of us." In fact, their speaking ill of us may be the measure of whether we're living out the hope we believe is impelled through us by the Word.

Laypeople live their call quite often without announcing it. Yet these unannounced answers to the call nonetheless go forward in hope. It builds and it builds, for each "going forward" signals more hope. And this is our signal in these days: don't despair. Live in the Lord; go forward in hope.

The classic signaler was John the Baptist. Like John, without fully understanding, we do what John did—we take up our vocation at God's urging. Here's what can be confusing. We mustn't wait until we have the full program of what we're going to do all laid out before us. Our lives of Christian vocation are a work in progress, not a template.

It is enough that the urge to do the work wells up—that it bubbles, springlike. It doesn't have to make complete sense. It certainly didn't make sense to John the Baptist. Years after he'd baptized Jesus he was still asking Jesus, "Are you the one?" To do what God wants, things don't necessarily have to make complete sense. God has to make sense of our efforts, and can, if we leave space for others to fill in what's intended. Others can write in what's missing from our best efforts.

This broader sweep, this not waiting until everything we hope to do makes perfect sense, can accomplish more than minute planning. The work of the Spirit through us can be remarkably similar to how the essayist Lord Macaulay described Lord Byron's poetry: "The strokes are few, and bold." The Greek poet Hesiod who said, "Half is often more than the whole," can certainly be applied to Christian witness.

In contemporary Christian life, perhaps no modern prophet stumbled and bumbled at times as much as Henri Nouwen, whom his biographer Michael Ford calls a "wounded prophet." Yet Nouwen had an incredible impact. (The Spirit works very strangely and we do well not to try to box the Spirit in. The Curé d'Ars had a very soft voice that didn't carry beyond the fifth or sixth row of pews. But even the people at the rear of the church were converted by what he was saying.)

As with all homilies and spiritual writing (including the Scriptures) perhaps it wasn't so much what Nouwen said or wrote as it was what his readers and listeners read into his words. If Henri couldn't always make sense of himself—and he certainly couldn't boil water for coffee, turn on a washing machine, or even adequately organize clearing the table and washing the dishes—for many he made sense of God.

This is the work before us at this moment. To make sense of God for people. By doing what we feel called to do in Jesus' name, and not worrying too much about getting it perfectly right.

We—inadequate, timorous, uncertain us—are in the words of *Gaudium et spes* and those "whose hopes are set on a genuine and total emancipation of mankind" not just through human efforts alone but through "the Christ who died and was raised and can show the way." Like a child carrying a bunch of hastily plucked flowers and weeds—not certain which bit is which—we bring with us Christian teaching. We bring

Christ who knows all about our inadequacies, yet is reliant on us nonetheless.

How do we know we can do it—live Christ this way—when we're so timorous? Ask Timothy of the first and second letters to Timothy.

We turn to the little red wagon, Patience. Timothy, his contemporaries felt, was a bit too patient—a sort of cowardly lion among disciples. Timothy was considered not assertive enough. Let's face it, looking back we can see that Timothy had a couple of problems. One was Paul. Timothy was Paul's assistant and it would be difficult to appear assertive if you're walking in Paul's shadow. And yet Paul relied on Timothy for fifteen years, so the disciple must have been doing something right. Paul trusted him. God trusts us.

Paradoxically, we must act to live out the hope, yet be patient with ourselves.

Timothy speaks of Christ's "inexhaustible patience for all the other people who would later have to trust in him to come to eternal life" (1:16). The Jesuit poet Gerard Manley Hopkins understood:

> *Patience, hard thing! the hard thing but to pray,*
> *But bid for, patience is! Patience who asks*
> *Wants war, wants wounds, weary his times, his tasks;*
> *To do without, take tosses, and obey.*

We know that, like faith, hope glows brighter and warmer when it's fueled by mutual prayer and sharing, and support. One can be a lifelong optimist on one's own. To live in hope needs the reassurance of God, of others, to prevent it from souring into despair.

We can see where the thrust came from, the origin of the renewed hope. It was sparked by the world's Catholic bishops some thirty-five years ago. The same thing that has us plumbing our depths had the bishops plumb the church's depths. In December, 1965, the two thousand-plus bishops assembled for the Second Vatican Council gave the world what they had found: *Gaudium et spes* ("Joy and Hope"). *Gaudium et spes* begins the preface to the council document, *The Pastoral Constitution on the Church in the Modern World:* "The joy and hope, the grief and anguish of the men [and women] of our time, especially of those who are poor or afflicted in any way, are the joy and hope, the grief and anguish of the followers of Christ as well."

We're to be listening to the echoes in our hearts of the world's grief and anguish. We're to be Christians first. Alas, up to now, said the bishops, "there is a painstaking search for a better material world without a parallel spiritual advancement." See how far that's gotten us.

There is the tension and tragedy still with us, "we have not seen the last of bitter political, social and economic hostility and racial and ideological antagonism." But we hope to see "the last" of it. And we'll work as if we can bring about "the last" of it. There's an enormous energy to this patient Christian hope—the energy created by the belief that change is possible.

Sheldon Vanauken in *A Severe Mercy* (Harper-Row, New York, 1977, p. 100) describes what we're leaping to:

> *Our only hope: to leap into the Word*
> *That opens up the shuttered universe.*

4

Facing Fear with Love

The whole world fell away last night
Leaving you, only you, and fright.
—Jean Vanauken

A friend sent an e-mail that spoke of a dear cousin whose divorce had been bitter. The intervening years were for her a tortuous saga of struggling through financial hardship and every other hardship to raise a large family by herself, alone. The husband had walked out of the marriage into a life of considerable personal luxury and self-indulgence.

The couple's youngest son was killed at the World Trade Center. He was on the ninetieth floor when the building fell. The ex-husband went to the site as a volunteer, worked day after day seeking tangible evidence of their thirty-year-old son. A watch, a school ring. Anything. He searched until he fell ill. He found nothing. At the Mass for the son organized jointly by his friends, the ex-husband approached his former wife. He asked if they had suffered enough, and could she forgive him. Said the e-mail: "They embraced for the first time in twenty-five years. I could only think of Georges Bernanos's 'All Is Grace.' I have prayed for decades my cousin would find peace. And in the rubble that buried thousands of beautiful brave youngsters, God rose once again and brought peace."

"All Is Grace" is the final judgment of the dying priest in *The Diary of a Country Priest* (1936) by Bernanos (1888–1948). Love out of such evil as the ashes of the World Trade Center. This love is about being open to the possibility of love, and to love, and to accept love. We know, too, that love is in some way involved with facing evil, and acknowledging suffering, including the loss of a loved one.

If Everything Is Lost

If everything is lost, thanks be to God
If I must see it go, watch it go,
Watch it fade away, die
Thanks be to God that He is all I have
And if I have Him not, I have nothing at all
Nothing at all, only a farewell to the wind
Farewell to the grey sky
Goodbye, God be with you evening September sky.
If all is lost, thanks be to God.
For He is He, and I, I am only I.
—Dom Julian, O.S.B.

"Even Jesus did not explain suffering," writes Father Richard McBrien. "He endured it. In the resurrection his suffering and death acquired a meaning beyond themselves. Such meaning is not always, nor even often, apparent. Christ teaches us that suffering can have a meaning, or can acquire a meaning. We can learn from it. We can be ennobled by it. We can grow through it. For the God who encounters us in suffering is a God who knows suffering from the inside, as it were, in Jesus Christ. In the end, the problem of evil and of innocent suffering reveals as well as conceals the God of love."

Love coupled to loss. Love coupled to peace. Love and laughter. Love within charity. All of these are in the cupboard of our

Christ-heart, the cupboard we draw from in order to face fear. Sometimes what we take from the cupboard is just a tiny thing. A rosary even.

The Beads

Onyx, plastic, pearl and gold
The Beadsman a thousand Aves told.
I tell mine when the world feels cold.
Pay him a penny, pay him a groat
The Beadsman's thousand Aves: rote.
I finger mine in the bottom of my coat.

Plastic, pearl, gold and jade
The Beadsman a thousand Aves prayed.
I pray mine most when I'm afraid.
Pursed in leather, pocketed in cloth
I clutch mine tightest
when the plane takes off. (ACJ)

It's when we're afraid that we cling tightest to God—to the beads, to Jesus, to Mary.

These days we're clinging to "Faith, Hope, and Love." We're all realizing how fragile our individual existences are. For many this has come as a shock. This is particularly true for that segment of the American middle class that thought it could live in isolation and safety through hard work and following the rules. That such things are not guarantees might make us bolder about thinking whether the work we do is what we should be doing, whether the rules we follow are worth following. The answer might be "yes" to both implied questions. But even if the answer is "yes," the question is still worth asking.

Arthur writes:

You know, I've wondered many times about whether any homeless people were killed in the World Trade Center attack.

> Who would know? Was there someone just moving into a nearby available, unused doorway, with a nice, clean cardboard box rescued from a dumpster? A feeling of "Ahh! This'll do." A polystyrene cup ready to stand on the corner with when the crowds start pouring out at lunchtime. No less a life lost when the huge skyscraper segments landed, buried, burned things to a crisp.
>
> I wonder if there might have been an older man, maybe old like me, an immigrant who'd just that morning picked up a money-under-the-counter day job delivering flowers. Joyfully riding up to the ninety-first floor with them to brighten someone's day, and knowing there'd be some money in the pocket that evening. Then a bang louder than hell's doors closing.

Reflecting herself on what had happened in New York, Melissa, a friend in California, wrote to us noting:

> *It is not accurate to assume that September 11, 2001 had the same impact on all Americans. Those many who daily live aware of life's fragility, the marginalized, have they lessons for us? Psychologists have noticed a strange phenomenon among some depression and anxiety patients. Some have had a lessening of symptoms since the attack. Maybe they feel the rest of the world now understands the hyper-awareness of our mortality and fear. Those the patients already faced in their own minds. How do the middle school children in the bad parts of L.A. and Santa Ana have the courage to walk to school each day, knowing that a drive-by shooting could end their lives at any minute? How do their mothers, who know that gangs and violence have taken too many young people already, have the courage to let their children out the door?*

Bin Laden said he wanted the United States to feel the despair that those in the Middle East feel as a result of our actions as a nation. Perhaps he has succeeded in some measure. I wonder, though, if our suffering will help us understand the suffering of all the marginalized people in the world. Or, if it will turn us inward. We have closed ranks as a nation. The flags are out on all the front porches in the suburbs, and that makes us feel better. Unfortunately, bin Laden has made it easy for us. He has given us an enemy with a face to focus on, and we all seem happy to concentrate on this specific embodiment of evil. Will we spend our time looking for swarthy Middle Eastern villains in our midst and forget about the more vague evils of poverty, ignorance, and hunger that sit at the borders of our suburbs? Are those time bombs of our own making we choose to ignore? Where does love of life enter this picture?

Not through money.

The Giant's Causeway

So vortex-like doth wealth now draw all other feelings in,
Too much we calculate, and wealth becomes almost a sin;
We look upon the lovely earth, and think what it may yield;
We only ask for crops, not flowers, from every summer field.

The mind grows coarse, the soul confined, while thus
from day to day
We let the merely common-place eat what-might-be away:
Ah! better to believe, I trow, the legends framed of old—
Aught—anything to snatch one thought, from selfishness
and gold.

—Anonymous

Love, like faith, carries a price tag. It's rarely a financial price tag. And it is obvious that in Melissa's commentary and "The Giant's Causeway," the whole topic of "love" is like the pencil headed into the pencil sharpener—the deeper it goes the more pointed it becomes. The point of the point is that the opposite of love is not hate. That is too easy. The opposite of love is evil. And that is very hard to absorb, especially when we're looking at it on the page.

It's hard because we operate in a world "poisoned by sin and choked by indifference." The cost to us of operating in that world often is measured in personal doubt. We doubt we can embrace evil.

Dolores writes:

A wise monk once remarked to me that I was capable of committing all the violent acts that I so condemned in others. He wasn't minimizing the seriousness of the evil, just being realistic about how we are, in reality, deeply connected and participating in the world *together,* a world in which the wheat and the weeds grow side by side.

Where is God during the times of unspeakable horrors?

Menachem Rosensaft, a child of Holocaust survivors, addressed this question during the dedication of the Holocaust Museum in Washington, D.C. "God was with every Jew who told a story or a joke or sang a melody in a death camp barrack to alleviate a friend's agony. The incredible element in the horror is not the behavior of murderers, because that is pure evil. It is the behavior of the victims, people who shared their rations and offered comfort. God was with them." I would add that God was with those outside the camps, the righteous men and women who helped save a fellow human being.

And God was in the World Trade Center with the worker who helped his disabled office mate to laboriously negotiate

> the staircase out of the horror. God was with the firefighters who kept returning to the furnace in search of life. God was with all who in large and small ways safeguarded the core of human dignity in each other.
>
> There is a fifteenth-century fresco of the Holy Trinity in Florence, Italy, in the church of Santa Maria Novella. The figure of God the Father is directly behind the crucified Christ, and appears to be supporting the cross. There is a stricken look on the Father's face as if he were almost overwhelmed with the cruelty of it all. One can imagine God holding the cross of September 11, and the cross of the subsequent war: God, the essence of Reality, stunned and stricken yet again. But one can also imagine God's sigh of relief at the boundless acts of love and sacrifice.

We doubt that we can even understand the need to embrace the reality. That's fine, because we're grappling with large concepts. Remember, "Doubts can have two effects: although they can enervate and weaken faith, they can also try and test it. Catholics must not rest comfortably on their belief. They are called to suffer many a struggle of doubt." So wrote the joint authors Archbishop Paul Hallinan and the late Cardinal Joseph Bernardin.

They continued: "The need of our times is love, human love shot through with the splendor of divine love, love of God demonstrated and proven in daily contact with our fellow men [and fellow women]. Of this Christian love, Pentecost is the birthday, the Holy Spirit is its source, and the sacrifice of the Mass its insertion into lives which without it would be dry and dull, but with it can be fresh and rich and full of wonder" (*Days of Hope and Promise*, ed. Vincent A. Yzermans, The Liturgical Press, Collegeville, MN, 1973).

Father Richard McBrien leads us into how the church sees love—and evil. Then we'll ponder a moment the older word, "charity."

McBrien asks: "First, what does love mean? In English there is only one word; in Greek there are four. *Epithemia* is desire, with the connotation of lust. This is sexual love. (All love is, of course, sexual, but not all sexual action is loving.) *Eros* is the drive toward union with others which brings self-fulfillment. *Philia* is affectionate love such as that among brothers, sisters, and friends. *Agape* is total dedication and devotion to the welfare of the other, regardless of sacrifice and personal cost. Many experiences of authentic love by human beings will entail a proportionate blending of these four elements" (*Catholicism*, Winston Press, New York, 1980, p. 976).

Explains McBrien: "All of Jesus' moral teachings and those of the early church have been concentrated in the one commandment of love: love of God, love of neighbor (Mark 12:28–34, Matthew 22:34–40, Luke 10:25–37, Galatians 5:14, 1 John 3:23, 1 Corinthians 13). " 'And now faith, hope, and love abide, these three; and the greatest of these is love' (1 Corinthians 13:13). These three virtues are distinct but not separate. Love is a lived faith and a lived hope. The one virtue without the other two is radically incomplete, dead."

But the whole thing is dead unless we take this love out to people—we are to be preaching with our lives.

Well, we say, I'm not up to that. Henri Nouwen answers us with a remark about living in the L'Arche community with the mentally retarded: "L'Arche discovered me and I was invited to do something I wasn't prepared for" (Michael Ford, *Wounded Prophet: A Portrait of Henri J. M. Nouwen*, Doubleday, New York, 1999, p. 156).

God is "discovering" and "inviting" us all the time. We can never be fully prepared.

If we want to learn what it is we're to do, we have to do what the disciples did when Jesus said, "Come and see" (John 1:39). We have to go and see. As Christians we have no choice in the matter. Not really. This is answering with love the God of love. Our teachers are those around us. We learn from everything. John Henry

Newman said: "Persons influence us, voices melt us, looks subdue us, deeds inflame us."

This chapter is leading us, as Christians and Americans, where we don't want to go. To pursue love means pursuing evil. "Confronting" evil isn't enough for Christians. We have to understand evil. Not quite embrace it, but certainly empathize with it.

You see, unless we understand and empathize with the enormity of evil, we can't understand the enormousness of the love necessary to overwhelm it. If we can't grasp that enormousness, then what we're actually praying for may not be focused on the correct things. And if the prayer isn't properly focused, then our contemplation risks being speculative rather than regenerative.

McBrien comments that "evil, like a miracle, is power, but a power against life, not for it. That there is evil in the world is obvious," he writes, but "what this evil is in its core is not so clear. God wars against it, and we are called to participate with God in the struggle against its every form: social injustice, oppression, infidelity, dishonesty, etc. God sent his Son to save us from 'the power of darkness and of Satan' " (McBrien, ibid., pp. 328–31).

These are difficult concepts. We have to learn about love and sin, love and evil. We don't come fully taught.

Love, like evil, has many variations on its main theme. The older usage for love, "charity," meant among other things a Christian kindness not limited to passing out goods from a charity basket. Being charitable meant that one presumed good intentions and motives in the actions of others. "Charity begins at home" was a reprimand. Don't go out doing good for others where everyone can see you if you don't have the virtue of charity within your own four walls.

Charity (love) demands from us freedom from censoriousness. This charitable love insists on leniency, beneficence, and liberality. "Mercy," said Archbishop Hallinan, "is a strong component of the virtue of love." Christians work best when they work with all the gifts in their Christ-heart cupboard. Love, justice, and charity are inseparable gifts all in the one packet. "Isn't God a humanist, in the sense that humanity is the one and only object of his love?" asks Ruben Alves. "Isn't God's only concern the happiness of human beings? Isn't that the very epitome of God's will?" (*Frontiers of Theology in Latin America*, ed. Rosino Gibelini, Orbis, Maryknoll, NY, 1979).

But if we're doing things in love, can we be sure we're always doing the right thing in the right way? Are we necessarily fashioning a God-given answer to the question, Jesus' own answer to the problem? Did the Good Samaritan wonder if he was doing the right thing? He was committing himself to untold expense. But no more so than the innkeeper, who didn't know whether the Good Samaritan would return and settle any further account run up from caring for the injured man.

We're far more likely to find ourselves in the role of the innkeeper than that of the Good Samaritan, wondering if we can trust. The Good Samaritan's love here was open ended, its outcome uncertain. But if we're the innkeeper, we might be participating in a gesture and commitment that will come back to haunt us. We might be making a *mistake!* Mistakes must not be confused with failure. Mistakes frequently are our own fault. Failure when we're attempting something out of faith as part of our Christian witness is something else again. For the Christian, failure is as welcome as success. That can't be said of mistakes.

The American Quaker Yardley Warner (1815–1885), known as "the Freedman's Friend," quoted in the book of that same name by his son, Yardley Warner (Wessex Press, 1957, p. 250), is aboard a ship headed from England to America when he makes this entry in his journal: "This evening, with all the light and warning of the past two days, I have sinned again with my tongue in uttering too much. Oh, that this may serve as a renewed humbling lesson to keep me low, and put me more than ever on the watch. I had a token of favor, too, just before that slide back into an old trap of the evil one—my vain love of approbation. But I seem to feel pardoning mercy extended to meet my efforts at watchfulness."

Perfection, Perfection

I have had it with perfection.
I have packed my bags,
I am out of here.
Gone.

As certain as rain
will make you wet,
perfection will do you
in.

It droppeth not as dew
upon the summer grass
to give liberty and green
joy.

Perfection straineth out
the quality of mercy,
withers rapture at its
birth.

Before the battle is half begun,
cold probity thinks
it can't be won, concedes the
war.

I've handed in my notice,
given back my keys,
signed my severance check, I
quit.

Hints I could have taken:
Even the perfect chiseled form of
Michelangelo's radiant David,
squints,

the Venus de Milo
has no arms,
the Liberty Bell is
cracked.
—Father Kilian McDonnell, O.S.B.

This business of failure and making mistakes is greatly misunderstood—even by many Christians.

We are to do as Yardley Warner did, apologize for our mistakes and guard against them. But where failure is concerned we should, in the final analysis, be unconcerned. (Who was a bigger failure than Jesus? He failed to convince, and was killed at the height of his powers.) As Christians acting out of their understanding of what God wants from us we are not called upon to succeed. Christians are called on to "do." Whether it is successful or not is in God's hands, not ours.

Essayist and scholar Louis Dupre says that "religion's most significant but least appreciated contribution in dealing with moral striving may well consist in assisting us in dealing with failure. Religion [works] on both sides of the moral scale: inspiring heroism at the top and consolation at the bottom. Both are equally essential. [As for failure], as G.K. Chesterton understood: 'If a thing is worth doing, it's worth doing poorly' " ("Secular Morality and Sacred Obligation" in *Riding Time Like a River: The Catholic Moral Tradition Since Vatican II*, ed. William J. O'Brien, Georgetown University Press, Washington, DC, 1993, p. 56).

Now, back to the present—and facing fear with love. We cannot, must not, overlook "the sobbing mess" that is coldly inflicted terrorism. We cannot, must not, overlook the Jesus who says: "Come to me, all you that are weary and are carrying heavy burdens, and I will give you rest. Take my yoke upon you, and learn from me; for I am gentle and humble in heart, and you will find rest for your souls. For my yoke is easy, and my burden is light" (Matthew 11:28–30).

W. H. Auden was talking of World War II ("In War Time"—June, 1942) when he caught the mood of the present day:

> *Those accidental terrors, Famine, Flood,*
> *Were never trained to diagnose or heal*
> *Nightmares that are intentional and real.*
> —(*The English Auden, 1927–1939,* ed. Edward Mendelson, Random House, New York, 1977, p. 461)

How does Jesus' yoke help face the intentional nightmares? A yoke is a device that harnesses two animals together to share the load. Jesus is not saying that we'll share his load, but that he'll share ours, half it, relieve it, and provide us with some company along the journey as well.

We don't undertake our particular vocation as Christians alone. Jesus is pulling with us, not just for us. "There are many kinds of charism," writes Jean Daniélou, "but love alone is the important thing. Vocation is a free gift; a particular vocation is something personal. It is a summons coming from a personal God to a human person. It expresses the essential character of the Christian view of things: a universe dominated by the reality and the value of the person." A reality dominated by a duo: Jesus yoked to us; us yoked to Jesus. Jesus carrying better than half the load.

Dolores writes:

An ancient stream of thought in Catholic Christianity has to do with how one person's suffering is redemptive for another. Thomas Aquinas explains it this way: "Further, since what we can do through our friends we somehow can do ourselves.

Because friendship takes two people (who are) one in affection, and particularly when the affection is charity. Therefore, just as one can justify one's own sins, so can one satisfy to God for another's. For the pain that a friend endures for another is taken, considered, by the other as though he himself were suffering" (from an unpublished paper by William Walsh, S.J.).

Not one of us, as Americans, has reacted in quite the same way to the horrifying events of September 11. Concepts of fear, terror, worry, anxiety, while sharing their familiar emotional content among all, are individual in how we personally react to them. So when Aquinas says, "For your friend to suffer is for you to suffer," it means that you understand much, but only God understands all of the friend's suffering.

"For a friend," continues Aquinas, "a friend's sufferings are his own. And consequently, the sufferings of Christ, contemplated by the sinner who is moved by charity, are at once an incentive to his love of God and the cause of the greatest sorrow for his own sins" (Walsh, same source).

Reading these words of Aquinas I am drawn to think of intercessory prayer as an act of love.

These are times, facing fear, when we are drawn to intercede on behalf of all those we love, whom we want to protect. If love is giving one's time and energy to another, then intercessory prayer certainly fits. Moreover, the motivation is often the bridge of empathy that moves us into the experience of another, our friend, whose pain we do, indeed, feel. It seems to me that the first and perhaps foundational move to make, as an act of love, is to turn to the God who loves and sustains us all, to ask for healing, insight, courage, peace—whatever our friends might need according to our own insights on the situation.

The ultimate prayer movement, however, is to turn our friend over to the loving embrace of God, who knows better than we what's needed. The point is that the primary movement of love for a friend (and doesn't Jesus, in the New Testament, hold up friendship as the quintessential relationship in the community he calls together?) is to share in the pain (and the joy) of another.

Evelyn Underhill, one of the twentieth century's more luminous writers on the spiritual life, holds up the connection between intercession for others and the willingness to act on their behalf. This means that as we pray for the alleviation of another's loneliness, for example, we are willing to visit that person, or write a letter, or connect in some tangible way.

Perhaps this thought was in the subconscious of "The Grandmothers." We are a small group of women "of a certain age" (to echo the novelist Barbara Pym). The Grandmothers have known each other for decades. In youth we met as a prayer group to steer us through the shoals of motherhood and citizenry. As we've grown older, our horizon has grown—now the world (including, of course, our grandchildren) is in the forefront of our consciousness.

In the week immediately following September 11, three of the Grandmothers, in between extensive volunteer commitments and ongoing professional life (although admittedly at a slower pace), picked up on a local news story about Muslim women being afraid to leave their homes. They were afraid to go out in their customary dress (headscarves) to perform their ordinary, everyday activities, like shopping. We wrote to the local mosque, identifying ourselves as members of a nearby Catholic church, and offering ourselves as "escorts" for the women. The imam read the letter to the congregation and let it be known that companionship was available.

Why did we do this? I think Aquinas's insight was present within us. We easily imagined ourselves in a similar situation, trying to care for our families and blocked because of fear. Our purpose, in a simple act of shopping, was to alleviate the fear that we, too, could feel.

As I signed the letter I remembered a similar feeling a few years earlier. I awoke to the clock radio and an account of a family in Sarajevo: a mother, a father, and two teenage children. The mother was a photographer, the father a businessman. The story described their high-rise apartment in great detail. I sat upright in bed. It could have been my apartment: the views, the rooms, the rhythms of high-rise living.

The Sarajevo family's apartment now was in ruins. They had been under bombardment for months, and now they were without jobs, the schools were closed, they were breaking up furniture for fuel. I felt then and I feel now the piercing power of John Donne's words: "Do not ask for whom the bell tolls / It tolls for thee" ("Meditation 17," *Devotions upon Emergent Occasions,* 1624).

Of course. The bell in Sarajevo was tolling for me. A quirk of geography was the only difference. Now, with terror our daily fare, there is not even the quirk of geography. My apartment is not in ruins, but it is close to where the plane crashed into the Pentagon—a distance that could have easily been overshot by that plane.

The Spirit that sustained the family in Sarajevo is the same Spirit that hovers over the smoking chasm that once was the World Trade Center, that hovers over the Pentagon, over the field in Pennsylvania, over the post offices of America—over all the world, including the small portion of it where I dwell.

O Spirit of the Living God, fall afresh on all of us.

5

Facing Fear with Family and Community

The trials, with which in recent months the Lord has tested my patience, have been many—anxieties, frustrations, disappointments, restrictions, interior discontent. Until now I have succeeded in holding this under control: all this—all this—makes it easier for me to enjoy the sense of trust and abandonment which contains also the longing for a more perfect imitation of my divine Model.

—Angelo Roncalli (later, Pope John XXIII)

Angelo Roncalli (1881–1963) was lonely when he wrote these words. He was living in a large house with a priest who was a little unbalanced. Angelo had grown up with lots of family. He understood family. He never ceased to pay tribute to his brothers whom he left behind, still tilling the family fields.

We have our own such images. And we have incredibly supportive morals and lessons that spring up from family—unbidden.

Reflection on Mark 10:13–16

Lazy Sunday afternoon,
folding laundry,
children scattered about the house,
reading, playing.
Door bell ringing—
neighbor informing me her huskies
have just mauled our cat.

Running, finding, carrying, calling for help—
the cat dying in front of all four girls
while I'm talking on the phone with the vet.
Two hours of wailing, holding—
learning a first hard lesson
in how suddenly life comes pouncing,
blindsiding,
wrenching hearts with loss.

Writing letters of farewell,
burning letters of memory into a crosspiece,
circling a gravesite in the woods,
holding hands,
the girls praying for their "Princess,"
I praying that my princesses will be safe
in this husky world.

Returning from the woods,
holding hands,
Elisabeth, all of 4,
Saying unbelievably:
"Dad—let's go forgive the dogs
that killed our cat."
—Kevin Anderson

Arthur writes:
We don't like to think about suffering. We're not very good at dealing with it. When suffering comes we get angry. Or, we're puzzled by it. Or, we're sad about it and the first question usually is: Why me? And the second: How do I deal with it? And the third: When will it go away?

Prayer comes into all the answers regarding suffering, as does patience. Angelo Roncalli is saying in the opening quotation that when we suffer, we seem to have less dynamism, not more; less patience, not more, just when we truly need it.

Where we can best bolster our diminishing strength is drawing from the energies of those around us—family and community. And we have a right to their support. Yet we have to draw from them without wearing them out or wearing them down, with the details of our suffering, singular or multiple. When we suffer we have to find a new balance in our lives. Yet we liked and prefer the old balance.

Right now we have to yank ourselves free of presuppositions. We're all suffering, for example, from the effects of September 11: fear of flying, or fear of anthrax poisoning, fears associated with ever-present uncertainties.

Suffering and grief, recovery and generosity are intertwined. Since the attack on the World Trade Center, we have seen evidence of families and the immediate communities drawing closer, being more supportive. It may not last—but we have seen it.

Let's examine the expectations others have of us through the prism of grief, as Linda Studniarz does.

Studniarz is a lay preacher at the St. Stanislaus Kostka Catholic community in Bay City, Michigan. The parish has between fifty and seventy funerals a year and Studniarz, a fifth-generation member of the parish, preaches at the vigil service for practically all of them. Certainly, at least once a week. She has keen insights on both grief and responsibilities.

"Grieving," she says, "is the most personal yet the most universal emotion. We all know what that emotion is like. So whether we've lost one person that we love, or lost five thousand as a country, I think the connection is very close. I believe that our country is going through a very deep grieving process. I wake up each morning and I dread turning on the TV because I don't know what I'm going to hear next. The person grieving has an absolute right to expect the support, understanding, and compassion of the circle of people around the grieving ones. And we have Jesus in Matthew 28:20: 'I am with you always, even until the end of the age.' "

Arthur writes:

As an aside on this business of people having an "absolute right" to call on us, I accept that almost without equivocation.

We lived on a cul-de-sac that ran into another short street before reaching the stop sign at the main road. On that short street lived a woman who had been severely injured in a car crash. She could not drive, indeed she could walk only with difficulty. She lived alone.

If she needed to go somewhere—and she usually went to a small restaurant about a half-mile away for lunch—she'd stand out in the short street and wave down any neighborhood car headed toward the stop sign. She'd tell them she needed a ride to wherever it was she needed a ride to. And the neighbors would take her. Wherever she was she used the same method to return home.

Some neighbors, some people in the restaurant, resented her demands. Others didn't. I didn't because I believed she had to right to call on us and our time and our transportation.

Linda Studniarz, presiding over a wake service, equally reminds us that it is in community, especially around the coffin, that we are moved to more fully love. As we grieve, or as we fear for our loved ones, we have to replant ourselves. Family and community provide the support that keeps grief from being despair. From them we learn again that we must send our Christian roots down deeper, into that humus of nourishment that is Scripture and Catholic tradition. Like the motorists on the short street confronted by my ex-neighbor, we must yield to the demands the facts place before us and act—and move from grief to joy.

The English priest and writer Father Ronald Knox (1888–1957) talked about this simultaneous grief and joy condition quoting Luke 6:21: "Blessed are you who weep now, you will laugh [for joy]." It happens at funerals, once people return from the cemetery and gather to reminisce.

With the shadows of September 11 metamorphosing into a gray-black terror perched like an evil bird on the shoulder of our inner thoughts, we need laughter in our grief. Many saints—Father Knox mentions Thomas More and Philip Neri as two—were merry folks in company. Knox drew a lesson for our times:

"The ordinary Christian," he said, "is less than a Christian if he is content to shrug his shoulders over the wickedness of mankind and ask what else you could expect. The mourner who has lost a dear friend will do his best to keep a brave face in company, but he would be less than human if there were not a sense of bitterness tugging at his thoughts. And the Christian is less than a Christian if he does not remember Jerusalem in his mirth."

In our fear and anxiety we're trying to do more than keep a brave face for company. We're trying to get so close to Jesus that uncertainty is an acceptable normalcy. Bitterness, like anxiety, is something we have to override. We can, we can. Because we have in the faith community what those who find God solely in their solo spirituality also would find solace in—as mentioned earlier—the community of communion: the Eucharist.

Yet we can't let the bitterness Knox refers to go unnoticed. Is the bitterness of life not having meant anything—in that we have no monuments to bequeath? We're nothing when we're gone!

With luck in life, the family provides the love, the faith community, the spiritual reassurance and courage, the neighborhood, the sense of belonging, and the political community provides the sense of security.

We as individuals are at the core of our own community. There's a giant stride of difference between being individuals and being individualistic. Archbishop Hallinan reminds us of this. He also signals that the community is to be as active in witnessing to Christ's love as is the individual. And we are to make it so: "We need to be lifted out of our individualism to catch a glimpse of the grandeur of our work in the church" (Hallinan, ibid., p. 15). It is a grandeur built of everything from mysticism to the communion of saints.

We don't have to explain it; we can simply accept it. Accept what theologian Dorothee Soelle is pointing to when she says: "We are surrounded by a cloud of witnesses. There is a mystical tradition, teaching and communicating itself, that excludes nothing and no one." Even—or especially—around the coffin, we are being taught. Even as we discuss the events of September 11 and after, we are being taught.

And we don't know in advance by whom.

It is in excluding "nothing" and "no one" from those who might teach us that we begin to understand things a little more clearly in the final three chapters of this journey. In the Family and

Community chapter, every *one* signals "God" to us. In the Prayer chapter, those we draw on signal God to us. In the Contemplation chapter, everything signals "God" to us.

We simply have to be something of the momentary mystic to let these facts penetrate. We have to permit the "God" in family and community to penetrate and influence us so we can be the "God" in family and community to others. Our role is that of Mr. Holland the music teacher in *Mr. Holland's Opus*, where one of the former students says: "Each one of us is a better person because of you." We know that's only possible if we are a better person because of God, or a better person because we have drawn the lesson from someone else—from God in them.

Even the tiniest improvement toward being more like God is so difficult. It's worse than dieting. We knock off five pounds, relax a minute, and put on six. To help us keep our spiritual diet, the faith community becomes our spiritual Weight Watchers—we have to be in the place of faith, drawing on others of faith, first and constant. This is what those who have a personal spirituality, but no spiritual community, are lacking—the God in others to draw from.

Being a better person is not so easy. Sometimes the very family and community we're trying to draw on doesn't want us to change *that* much—because our change might challenge them more than they want to be challenged. So how do we handle that? By accepting the haphazard of everyone and everything in our life. Nothing is straight-line progress. We add a bit, we lose a bit; we add three bits and lose one and now we're ahead. Bits of Jesus and bits of the saints, yes—but equally so, bits we are learning from those immediately around us. They're the immediate "God" for us when we're not in church, not with faith community, not in prayer, and not contemplating.

Liturgy

Some days, I will skip daily mass,
And take up worship in the park.

Under cathedral vaults of sacred oak trees,
I will spread a crisp white napkin
Over a dingy splintered park bench,
While overhead, God orchestrates hymns with
Gently gusting winds through the canopy of leaves.

There is no lector, and so I sit in stillness,
Calling forth a litany of deeply buried Psalms
That rumble from my heart.
Inevitably from the river, the fisherman's bell
Will signal consecration.

Ignorant of rubrics, I unceremoniously break out
A baguette from my brown tabernacle sack.
Like Francis of Assisi I minister first to gulls,
Then to squirrels, who resound amen
With a flap of a wing, and a flick of the tail.

Then, homeless Ben crouches in front of me,
Concealing every bit of his holiness,
Crudely Ben polishes off the load,
And in a gruff reciprocal gesture, offers me
A swig from his nasty flask.

Bread and wine, body and blood. I find myself shaken
And so the proper wording of liturgy escapes me.
Meanwhile, in all his wildness, Ben watches and waits.
Reluctantly I close my eyes, purse my lips and
Take a quick burning sip.

Ah, the mystery of faith!
Definitely not a Guardini liturgy,
And yet it suffices.
—Sascha T. Moore

It's what we already know—what is God saying to me through this person that I may don more of God on my person? Have I the courage to accept what he or she offers?

God is present to us in all the categories of family and community. And, oh, how we love that familiarity! Just look at that word, "familiarity." It has "family" right in the middle of it.

Familiarity

Same old house, same old key,
Same old family, same old me,
Same old faces—
And same old aroma when
Glory be to God for—
I'm back in my home again. (ACJ)

The familiarity that is family is our best guard against mindless materialism. Usually those we love most in the family have the least.

Without the constant awareness that others from everywhere can offer us, like cookies on a tray, we'll not escape the artificial values of much of our society that swarm like locusts and nibble away our better judgment. Our overarching economic system is selfish, based on hedonistic personal gain. Materialism has us exploiting ourselves. Materialism "commodifies" us, values us by what we're worth, not by who we are or what we value.

Society places its highest priority on "things," not people. And we can be sucked into that. We can lose our detachment. We need a place to stand to see things better—our society, ourselves.

Sometimes the Scriptures give us that place. Sometimes the quiet calm after the Eucharist gives us place and space. Sometimes a beautiful musical phrase brings us to our senses. Sometimes a conversation. Sometimes the sight of someone, like Ben in the park. Sometimes just an awareness that catches us by surprise can alter our direction, put us back on course. Something or someone simply provides us with sufficient calm to sleep that night.

We dare not underestimate the gift of one day, and one night, at a time. It is all we have. The right now, the immediate. Life at this instant.

The table was frequently Jesus' gathering place. Do we gather family, friends, strangers at our table? The table is about sharing (food) and companionship (love). The table is an informal teaching place, an informal center of learning. At our table or the eucharistic table there are answers to some of our questions. Simply in having gathered. Who is at our table? As the Carmelite nun Sister Wendy Beckett remarked (she was talking about the burden of humanity, and it applies equally to living with tragedy and uncertainty): "We are not asked to bear the burden alone. We are asked only to realize we cannot bear it alone." This sounds like a family at Thanksgiving.

Dolores writes:

November never fails to stir my inner world. All kinds of contrasting feelings surface as leaves assume their glorious hues and then fall silently to earth, leaving behind bare branches that eventually resemble black webs against the sky. Both my parents died in the month of November, as did my eighth-grade teacher, Sister Edith, who was an enormous influence in my adolescence and throughout my adult life. The memory of Sister Edith reading aloud to her assembled class from Washington Irving's *Sketch Book* often moves me in autumn, in November, to return to "Rip Van Winkle" with its vivid description of the terrain. It's a happy moment in the midst of sad memories of loss.

So is Thanksgiving. Each year this "holy holiday" looks a little different in our home—different family members, different friends. The difference enriches the experience. This year, "the year the world changed," I find myself reviewing past years, remembering those who have shared Thanksgivings with us, especially those now gone to God. There's Moira, an English woman, single, who worked as a freelance editor. One year, she let it slip that she would be having dinner alone at a local cafeteria, albeit an upscale one. Thereafter, Moira always joined us for the feast until cancer created an empty place. A priest friend, a gifted canonist, sometimes joined us. Recently, congestive heart failure stopped his ever-generous heart. After my brother Joe's death in 1981, his wife frequently made a Thanksgiving visit. She would arrive with piles of piano music, and her exquisite recipe for gravy, southern style. Now, she too is gone, another victim of cancer.

They are gone, but in some sense still intimately present as I anticipate Thanksgiving at the beginning of the twenty-first century. An old friend from Brittany, along with her three young adult children, will be with us, and I rejoice to think of the animated conversation that is likely to ensue. Bretons tend to be argumentative (in a friendly sense), and my friend, like my family, loves political discourse, so strong opinions are likely to be passed around with the sweet potatoes. I find the prospect comforting. It says to me that some things will not change, no matter what.

Our family, from generation to generation, loves to cook (and eat), and enjoys politics and politics' next of kin, religion. This will go on even as we remember those we love

> whose physical presence we no longer enjoy, even as we remember and relive our national vulnerability. Shared words, from conversation to table prayers, shared bread (at home and at the altar), shared laughter and music—I am strengthened by all these ordinary sacramentals. From seventeen-year-old Sam who wants to be a writer to three-year-old Grace who is always full of smiles, I see how loving the future is. There is still violence as the war against terrorism continues, and this makes for a heavy heart. But our young have a way of lightening the burden.
>
> It's like November, full of color as well as darkness. It's like the insight of Saint Therese, "tout est grace."

Jesus led us toward a new kind of solidarity. He didn't expect us to walk into this trap of befriending our anxieties—or the needy—alone. He's always on about our neighbors, and children. Plural not singular. He thought and taught about the responsibility of the individual in the context of the group. It is in this new group of believers—the Christians see how they love one another, says Tertullian—that we meet the neighbor, and the oppressed and the marginalized, and the fearful and scared. We meet ourselves.

A mother whose son died of AIDS wrote: "Christ's love has come to me through the caring and compassion I have received from others. Seek and accept the comfort of others whom you feel are helpful to you. We do not 'get over' grief; it is a process we must walk through."

Whether dealing with tragedy or fear, grief or continuing uncertainty, we need to know, too, that we're not going to behave perfectly. We're not going to achieve everything we hope to achieve, not even with the support of the family and the community. But we can do what we can do. Yardley Warner spoke to just this point in 1872. What he said has an antiquated ring to it, but that detracts nothing from his sincerity.

Remember the will to do rightly,
If used will the evil confound;
Live daily by conscience that nightly
Your sleep be peaceful and sound.
In contests of right never waver—
Let honesty shape every plan,
And life will of Paradise savor,
If you do as near right as you can.
—Yardley Warner (ibid.)

We can't get close to doing right if our starting point is individualism. The Canadian priest Father Daniel Donovan, in *Distinctively Catholic* (Paulist Press, Mahwah, NJ, 1997), remarks on the tendency of "secular life to push religion into the sphere of the private and the personal." Church becomes a gathering place of the like-minded, but not a community. "Whatever the causes of religious individualism," says Donovan, "it is profoundly at odds with much that is central to the traditional understanding of Catholic identity. The community of believers, the church, is at the heart of the Catholic faith."

Archbishop Hallinan spoke of the "tremendous spiritual effect" of Christians who "bear Christ in their lives" out into the unhearing, uncaring secular society. It is in this secular society that the church, not just the individual, is to serve as "a catalyst, as the conscience of society." It is too much to do alone. We confront fear just as we face the world, by entering into the world—with others, with faith, with hope, in love.

It was with the entire world in mind that the Catholic bishops from all over the world urged the Catholic community into modern society with all its ills and needs, whether they were haunting us personally or not. The Vatican II document *The Pastoral Constitution on the Church in the Modern World*, said Hallinan, "reads like a healthy commentary on the hopes and anguish of our world and a spiritual prognosis for its improvement." Real renewal cannot come out of a vacuum. It is formed by present needs and fresh insights. But it must draw its strength chiefly from the God-guaranteed treasures: "I will be with you all days." As television coverage takes us into the anguish of our world—with pictures of much of the Islamic and Arab world's crushing and ever-continuing poverty, we understand what the phrase "fresh insights" can actually mean. We are being given eyes to see.

The call to us in family and community is clear—to produce Catholic witnesses to the pain of the world, including our own pain. But more truly the pain of others. And perhaps, their pain first. We must produce "Catholic witnesses and not nominal Catholics, nor safe Catholics, not comfortable Catholics, not well-to-do Catholics, nor famous Catholics. The urgent need is the Christian witness, and in numbers large enough to make their presence felt."

If the tragedies of September 11 are causing us as individuals to thrust deeper to unearth the faith, insight, and courage Hallinan talks about, can we help our family and community and our church to also thrust deeper? Right now, in these anxious times, we need all that Christianity offers to produce Christian witnesses in numbers large enough to make their presence felt.

John the Baptist "established a community of those preparing" for baptism, and expected they would continue as a community once they had received the Spirit. Jesus asked John to admit him to this community preparing for baptism. That's our community, the very same community, the identical community of the baptized that Jesus wanted admission to in order to lead it to God. Neither baptism nor Jesus suggested that this would be a safe trip. Nonviolent themselves, they were dealt with violently.

What consolation did Jesus offer them, and us? Another John tells us what Jesus told them: "I am the way, and the truth, and the life. . . . Peace I leave with you; my peace I give to you. I do not give to you as the world gives. . . . If anyone believes in me, even though he dies he will live . . ." (John 14:6, 27; 11:25).

And Jesus asked: "Do you believe this?"

They did.

We do. In life beyond life, in a peace the world cannot give.

Here is a short, and slightly changed, excerpt from a Celtic prayer that appears in full later.

And I beseech Thee
To shield me from sin,
To shield me from ill,
To bless me this night,
Though I am not poor,
O God of the poor!
O Christ of the wounds
Give me wisdom along with Thy grace.

Up to this point we have said little enough about ourselves as Americans and Catholics. Let's take the briefest of excursions into history to remind ourselves of the religious freedoms we have because of the fact that we live where we live.

We take this excursion, as we pray and reflect, to remind ourselves that while we are not exceptional, we are different. And we're materially blessed. "Though I am not poor, / O God of the poor!" applies to most of us. Jesus has many words and pointers as to what our relative wealth and comforts demand of us on a world scale, for the world is our contemporary community. And our contemporary community, Jesus tells us, is what will get us into heaven.

The Vatican II council fathers urged us Catholics to enter the world. How does the immediate world—our nation—look?

United States civil society of the past two centuries has always carried a big stick. Periodically, it has noticed religion in its path in the public square, tossed religion up in the air like a ball, and thwacked it out of the park. Periodically, just like kids playing outside the ballpark, events like those of September 11 insist that the topic of religion be tossed up again and whacked back into the square. Whatever religion is about to do in the public square, let it do it and see what happens. At best, it might even catch on. The best argument for Christianity—and the worst—is Christians.

The nineteenth-century Catholic Archbishop John Ireland said of Americans: "We are not all of one mind upon religion and social questions: indeed, upon many matters we are at variance. But we know one another, and we love liberty. We take as our rule to grant to others what we wish to have for ourselves. We never use the law to enforce our own personal ideas. We respect others because we wish ourselves to be respected. We have our rights, and we freely concede the rights of others."

We don't use our law to enforce—but we must, Jesus says, use our personal example to persuade.

The Jesuit John Courtney Murray in the 1960s explored what was behind the idea of religious freedom that we enjoy in this country. It was, he said, the "common consciousness that considers the demand for personal, social and political freedom to be an exigency that rises from the depth of the human person. It is the expression of a sense of right approved by reason. It is therefore a demand of natural law in the present moment of history."

It isn't a freedom devoid of responsibilities, however. Our duty is to point out what is good and what is not in the nation. It's amazing how words uttered more than a century ago continue to reflect this sentiment. On a visit to Rome in 1887, and in words that resonate today, Cardinal James Gibbons of Baltimore (1834–1921) explained how American Catholics feel: "Without closing my eyes to our defects as a nation, I proclaim, with a deep sense of pride and gratitude, and in this great capital of Christendom, that I belong to a country where the civil government holds over us the aegis of its protection."

Three more elements then to weigh: the nation's defects, the deep sense of pride and gratitude, and the government as protector. (Cardinal Gibbons concluded his statement this way: "I belong to a country where the civil government holds over us the aegis of its protection—without interfering in the legitimate exercise of our sublime mission as ministers of the Gospel of Jesus Christ.")

We mustn't "close our eyes to our defects as a nation" because, as the world's wealthiest people, we must take up—according to Jesus' words and example—the life and lives of the poor. To be "poor in spirit" is not an incidental state of mind. It is the most profound demand Jesus makes of us. Jesus is saying that this spirit of poverty, coupled to being like little children, is how we balance the beam. How we join the larger community of saints in the life beyond life.

As Catholic Christians, why do we think that we can draw enough of us together to create a new moment? Our very overcoming of fear gives us this opportunity. If everyone is afraid and we're not, we'll be heard. The rest don't have to like everything about us to benefit from the fact that we're not afraid. Americans didn't like everything about the American revolutionary Thomas Paine (1737–1809) either. When Paine launched *The American Crisis* in 1776, the world first heard the phrase: "These are the times that try men's souls"—this was Paine's opening line.

It was the very recognition that this was so that gave hope to what was by that time a desperate cause. Equally so today, "these are times" to try the soul of every American man and woman. We can become the antidote to their desperation—providing we're as frank as Paine was (over slavery) about what the country and the world need as part of the antidote: food, education, health care, jobs, and freedom from oppression.

True, we can't predict that we'll be fully understood. But, in the unity of being Christians together, the broader community may well recognize in our mutually sustained courage the seed of communal resolve. Even those who vilified Tom Paine for his antislavery activities could see what was at work in his rallying words during different crises. We can provide the same service, providing that we're drawing on the support of our community, the communion of saints community.

Again, the nineteenth-century Quaker Yardley Warner shows where we find buoyancy in times of stress: "Burdens—sinking burdens—multiply—and from week to week I scarcely know what to hope for. But wonderfully comes the help, and the work goes on" (Warner, ibid., p. 236).

"Comes the help" from family and community. At times, we are the help that comes, the Catholic help. One hopes and trusts that Michael Novak is as correct today as he was a quarter-century ago when he wrote: "To be a Catholic is not so much to belong to an organization as to belong to a people. It is, willy-nilly, even without having chosen it, to have a differentiated point of view and sensibility, to have participated in a certain historical way of life." In the mainstream, but not totally of it, says Novak: "Catholics do tend to differ in their sense of ultimate reality, in their version of realism, in their particular passion for justice, in their sense of the meaning of family and children, in facing death, in their approach to education, to suffering and to personal relations."

We are facing fear with family and community as Catholics. This means that we face fear in a particular way.

Yet we give to family and community—to God too—in blindness, because whenever we move into action, we only know the general direction. We are required to give. We give of ourselves with generosity. We give at each step of the way. And everything we give we get back a hundredfold at the Eucharist.

Mouse Tale

Little by little now, or in a rush,
things leave me. Giving a little wave
as if they'll see me tomorrow. Only you,
with our thousand ties, denied me that.
So I conjure up a smile; it beams
out of somewhere and finds me when it can.

My heart grows wider, flatter
like the uncircled earth, with these
departures. I didn't know that walking
through a desert could feed you so,
thrust up cliffs and mesas beyond range
of cathedrals, lead to canyon rims
where you can peer
at cornfields and horses,
even birds with an eagle's eyes.

There is the tale of a mouse
who wanted to climb a mountain.
He gave one eye to a dying buffalo
and cross the plain beneath him,
then another to save a wolf,
and him blind to the mountaintop,
where an eagle seized him,
then far below he saw wolf, plain, buffalo.
He had become the eagle.

Death can mean that when we are eaten
by what we love.
—Justine Buisson

Today we don't know what, in love, we're going to give tomorrow.

We'll lean toward what Father Ronald Knox says: "within reason, give optimism the benefit of the doubt" (*Lightning Meditations*, Sheed and Ward, 1959, p. 84). It seems so commonplace, so ordinary.

How can we confront fear this way, using family and community as a shield while we're shielding family and community with our spirit? Because we've learned. We've discovered that in family life is the sacred mystery of God's presence, and that God and Spirit emerge from the very ordinariness of it all.

Thus fortified, we can abandon ourselves to God in trust, as did Angelo Roncalli.

> *For this reason I bow my knees before the Father,*
> *from whom every family in heaven and on earth*
> *takes its name.*
> *I pray that, according to the riches of his glory,*
> *he may grant that you may be strengthened*
> *in your inner being*
> *with power through his Spirit,*
> *and that Christ may dwell in your hearts through faith,*
> *as you are being rooted and grounded in love.*
> —Ephesians 3:14–17

6

Facing Fear with Prayer

Christians NEVER say goodbye!

—C. S. Lewis

Over the centuries, there have been—and still are—occasions around the world when Christian believers are forbidden to gather to pray. In addition, as in Afghanistan (or Pakistan) in October, 2001, this ban has made it dangerous to gather to pray.

In the nineteenth century, Alexander Carmichael (1791–1865), a Scotsman who collected orally the dying and obsolete incantations, hymns, words, rites, and customs of the highlands and islands of Scotland, referred to the dreadful effects of the Reformation on the Catholic islanders and highlanders of Scotland as "the reaction" (*Celtic Invocations [Carmina Gadelica]*, Vineyard Press, 1972, p. 37). As Carmichael went among the now elderly Catholics, the last survivors of a tradition, he took down their prayers. Over a dedicated lifetime of collecting, Carmichael has left us a quite beautiful testament to what prayer is, and a memory of how people once prepared for prayer:

> *Old people in the Isles sing this or some other short hymn before prayer. Sometimes the hymns and the prayer are intoned in low tremulous unmeasured cadences like the*

moving and moaning, the soughing and sighing of the ever-murmuring sea on their own wild shores.

They generally retire to a closet, to an outbuilding, to the lee of a knoll, or to the shelter of a dell, that they may not be seen or heard. I have known men and women of eighty, ninety and a hundred years of age continue the practice of their lives in going from one to two miles to the seashore to join their voices with the voicing of the waves and their praises with the praises of the ceaseless sea.

Rune Before Prayer

I am bending my knee
In the eye of the Father, who created me,
In the eye of the Son, who purchased me,
In the eye of the Spirit who cleansed me,
In friendship and affection.
Through Thine own anointed One, O God,
Bestow upon us fullness in our need,
Love towards God,
The affection of God,
The smile of God,
The wisdom of God,
The fear of God,
And the will of God
To do on the world of the Three,
As angels and saints
Do in heaven;
Each shade and light,
Each day and night,
Each time in kindness,
Give Thou us Thy Spirit.

—Alexander Carmichael *(Carmina Gadelica)*

The late spiritual guide and retreat master Jesuit Father Anthony de Mello (1931–1987) said he was always amazed when spiritual directors admitted difficulties in explaining to people how to pray: "This always amazes me because I have found it relatively easy to help people pray." De Mello based his teaching on some simple theories he followed in his own life, that it is legitimate to seek "fulfillment and satisfaction from prayer," and that "prayer is made less with the head than with the heart" (*Anthony De Mello*, Writings selected by William Dych, S.J., Orbis, Maryknoll, NY, 1999, p. 27).

Walking Humbly with God
(Three Haiku)

We think, therefore
We cannot relate
To our loving, compassionate God.

In letting go of all our worries
We allow God
To play a role.

Even our most profound
Innermost musings come
As pure gift from God.
—Vic Hummert

Continues De Mello: Most spiritual leaders "equate prayer with thinking. That is their downfall."

Prayer, says De Mello, is communication with God achieved mainly through the use of words; contemplation is the same communication by a different means—it is achieved "with the minimal use of words, images, and concepts, or dispenses with them altogether."

Arthur writes:
This business about not thinking in order to pray brings up again that issue of "presence." I'm reminded of two instances that illustrate what "presence" is, and does. I'm currently writing a biography of Pierre Toussaint, the former Haitian slave who lived in New York from the 1790s to the 1850s. There's an occasion when his dearest and closest friend loses a family member. From the records we do not know who the deceased is, only that Pierre's friend experiences profound grief. Toussaint goes to his friend's home. Later, another friend asks: "What did you say to her?" Toussaint replies that he did not say anything. There was nothing to say. He simply sat there with his friend and was present—totally present.

Secondly, a pastor told me that when he was ordained a priest he was younger than most. He had no sooner checked his bags into his first rectory than he was sent to console a prominent member of the parish whose spouse had just died. Like Toussaint a hundred years earlier, but much more hesitantly, the young priest went to the house, was taken to the family member, and took a chair next to him. Anxious, and not knowing anything about the man, or his spouse, or the family, in his wee terror he sat there for an hour, completely silent. Eyes closed. Then he gently touched the man's sleeve, stood, nodded to him and left. As my priest friend told it, for weeks afterward the family was telling his pastor what a fine and sensitive young priest he was, and how consoling at a time of grief.

No matter where we are, says De Mello, "God is already there. Our business is to recognize this." Father Anthony also wants to see the difference between what he calls Primary Cause and Secondary Causes—so he can apply our understanding to today.

"The Hebrews seemed to dwell almost exclusively on the Primary Cause," says De Mello. Were their armies defeated in battle? It was God who defeated them, not the ineptness of their generals. Did it rain? It was God who made the rain fall. Their view was partial," he says, for the Hebrews seemed to ignore secondary causes entirely.

The modern view of reality "is equally, and more grossly partial," he said, "for we seem to ignore the Primary Cause entirely. Has your headache disappeared? Where the Hebrew would have said, 'God cured you,' we say, 'Leave God out of this, the aspirin cured you.' The reality is that it was God who cured you—through the aspirin, of course. We have, however, all but lost our sense of the Infinite operating within our lives" (De Mello, ibid., p. 38).

Dolores writes:
I first began to read and "pray" the Psalms with a real inner commitment to let them speak to me the word(s) of God decades ago. When I did, I came up against the violence that weaves in and out of these great soul-songs. What was one to make of the desire for children to be smashed, to make one's enemies a footstool, to crush "the other" into nothingness? As I pondered and prayed, it seemed to me that the words were about the battle that was going on within, within me and within every soul on earth from the beginning to now—whenever "now" was. I found it interesting, therefore, to learn that "jihad" has an inner meaning, that it refers first to the deeper war going on within individuals and communities. It's beginning to look like the three monotheistic religions have some serious common ground to explore.

Catherine Madsen, contributing editor of *Cross Currents,* takes biblical violence in a slightly different (although related) direction. She writes: "God as he appears in the Bible is not so much goodness personified as the whole of life personified—what we love and what we dread, what we hope to do and what we would never do; it is an attempt to pack everything into one image, a synthesis of the lived and the unlived life."

Madsen's analysis is not unlike the description of God as ultimate reality. One of the reasons I've been drawn to the writings of Evelyn Underhill is her understanding of the mystical encounter. As a young woman, when I read in *Practical Mysticism* these words, "Mysticism is the art of union with Reality," I knew I had found a mentor. What I wanted was bedrock reality, something that would sustain me, direct me, correct me, lead me to the truth, in the various arenas of life: parenting, community politics, social justice, church work.

Perhaps what we have lost is the sense of God in the immediate. Before they put a flame to it, the Celtic islanders and highlanders blessed the kindling with which their fires were lit. Does it make any less sense for us to thank God when we turn on the electric light? God was everywhere and in everything—and still is!

If we tend to shy away from the immediate God, we tend to do the same with prayer.

Arthur writes:

When I open a box from the store with something new in it—I recently bought a camera, for example—I ask God to bless all who have handled it and its packaging and its transportation. Especially because I suspect many of those who touched it along the way are underpaid.

I do the same when I'm cooking and handling the vegetables and fruits. I pray for the farmers at the farmers market, the migrants who pick my tomatoes.

It isn't much, and I don't always remember. But I try to.

To my everlasting embarrassment (offset by ease of assembly), we own at my urging an artificial Christmas tree made in China. Embarrassment aside, each year, when I retrieve the tree from the loft and assemble it, those factory workers who made it are in my prayers. I try hard to make the connection, through prayer, with the people behind the things and services that make my life easier and more convenient.

And I try to use my smile as a prayer. Even when I don't feel like it I'm always nodding to people as I go past them on the street, greeting people in the supermarket, opening a cheery conversation with the person next in line in the post office. Sometimes I'm misunderstood. Sometimes I get the cold shoulder. But most times people are pleased to have a little fleeting brightness and a smile themselves with the person next in line.

I call my effort a prayer.

It isn't much, a smile. But it's me being me. I believe this is what God is asking of us: to be our best selves as best we can, and to make life the prayer.

Sometimes it is so hard to make prayer come that we shouldn't try. Hamlet worried, "My prayers fly up, my thoughts remain below." De Mello tells us that to be at prayer is to pray, too. God knows. That's all. And that's enough, if we can accept that it is enough.

Morning Prayer

Thanks be to Thee, Jesus Christ,
Who brought'st me up from last night,
To the gladsome light of this day,
To win everlasting life for my soul,
Through the blood Thou didst shed for me.

Praise be to Thee, O God, for ever
For the blessings Thou didst bestow on me—
My food, my speech, my work, my health.

And I beseech Thee
To shield me from sin,
To shield me from ill,
To bless me this night,
Though I am not poor,
O God of the poor!
O Christ of the wounds!
Give me wisdom along with Thy grace.
—Alexander Carmichael (ibid., p. 8)

Prayer is pushing itself upon our consciousness—even when we don't want it, even when we'd prefer to sleep.

Insomnia

The prayers for which no words will come
When tides of love have left me dumb—
Lord, God, in their stead accept
Unwilled vigils—willingly kept.
—Sister Janet Benish, O.C.V.

The trauma inflicted upon all of us on September 11, 2001, is our love being tested—love of God, love of fellow beings, even love of those who perpetrated this cruel, criminal act. As in a marriage or a starting relationship, love doesn't become strong until it is tested. We try to think these things through and find ourselves completely in the dark. We haven't lost faith. We haven't lost hope. We know there is love. But we're bewildered by the way God does things and in prayer, sometimes, we try to sort out the bewilderment. "The only recourse," says Jean Danielou, "is to have faith in its absolutely pure state: to have recourse to him who is the very source of faith."

And if this requires a miracle on our part, so be it.

How Easily a Miracle

How easily a miracle happens:
everything falls into place.
No distant thunder,
much less lightning,
walks the sky.
No deus shifts the gears
in machina.
All pain, or fear, or loss
becomes irrelevant.
The hoped for happening at once
seems pre-ordained,
inevitable,
comfortable
as a pearl cupped in the palm of my hand,
natural
as bloom from bud,
quiet
as an unparched lawn,
a pillow on which to rest
and rise again.

How long before Lazarus complained
his porridge was cold?

—Margaret Doyle

That lovely, witty, wonderful nun on television, Carmelite Sister Wendy Beckett, the art commentator, says that in prayer "there are no norms, no rules, no prohibitions as such. All prayer demands that we look at good (which usually demands we look at nothingness, God being pure Spirit and unconfinable in any image), and *do what seems to work.*"

There is the prescription. Do what seems to work.

Sister Wendy sets us straight: "Prayer is the only human action where cheating is impossible. Whether our response is working or not—whether it is a way into love or an escape into self—only we can know. If it seems right, it will be right. As soon as pretense sets in, prayer stops."

She explains that God never ceases to look at us, but "needs our consent if His love is not to be powerless."

Prayers of Beige

Prayers of beige
were muted
like sky with cloud
like cool without wind.

The limits of beige
dulled all tones.
All utterance rose tired
and fell under its sandy weight,
without giving up a cloud
leaving no puff of smoke
as signal.

But it was heard,
still small tracing to
center of black
womb-matrix
and red was born.

And purple was exulted
and orange was alleluia.

Every soul hears the color of its prayer.
—Jeannie Bench

Now we are secure in the knowledge that whatever we do as prayer is prayer. We see, first, that we make each color our prayer according to who we are. Next, we take the point about prayer opened by Father De Mello—presence.

Dolores writes:
The critical first step in prayer is simply to begin. If we want to talk as we pray, that is fine, but we must also listen. We have to hear the human needs we're praying about, the human needs that touch and sometimes break the heart of Christ. As we listen—if we listen—we are directed to join our will to God's will. If we take our listening power into the Scriptures, the Psalms, what joy we can find! I'm forever grateful, when it comes to prayer, to the Benedictines and the Jesuits.

To the Benedictines I am indebted for their handing on the tradition of the *lectio divina* (the divine lesson). This is the form of prayer in which one chooses a passage of Scripture, reads it through, and then reads it again, slowly and attentively, stopping when a word seems to arrest attention. There is the sense that the Scripture passage, the living Word of God, has initiated a conversation.

To the Jesuits I'm grateful for preserving and teaching Saint Ignatius' imaginative way of scriptural prayer, when we experience an inner encounter with Jesus. Many find the letters of Paul a springboard into prayer. That writer's heartfelt prayers often are not unlike the heart-prayers of many a parent.

One element strikes me as essential in prayer. It is listening. I have the conviction that prayer and Christian creativity are closely allied. I saw clearly in my research into the life of Jessica Powers, the Carmelite poet (*Winter Music,* Theological Book Service, 1992), that her life as poet (before her entrance into the monastic life) was, in fact, a disciplined way of life which perfected her capacity to be open and transparent. She was always looking and listening. She often focused on listening.

The point of all listening is, of course, to listen to God. Our Scriptures are filled with accounts of searching people listening for the Divine Voice (much as we are searching now). You remember Elijah (in the First Book of Kings) who sought God. God told Elijah to stand on the mountain and the Lord would pass by.

What happened?

There was nothing but thunder and lightning. God was not there. Next came a mighty wind, but God was not there either. And then an earthquake, followed by a fire. Still, no God. Then, Scripture says, "There was a tiny whispering sound. When he heard this, Elijah hid his face in the cloak" (1 Kings 19:11–13). He knew, then, the presence of the Lord. Some translations use the term "sheer silence" instead of "whispering sound." In sheer silence, too, we hear.

So how do we listen to God?

We do so, certainly, in the experience of silence, one of the most primal experiences. Silence is not notable in our culture, one cluttered with talk shows, evening news chatter, headphones, city cacophony. Some people use Lent for a "media fast." I can attest that it helps clear out the spiritual arteries. "Prayer before the morning paper" is becoming our household motto. A silent radio is a form of blessing.

We also listen to God in the Scriptures. There is a word addressed to you, to me, personally. The ancient prayer form of *lectio divina* is still very much practiced.

For instance, you might think of any Psalm that has touched you, and look at it again today. See if different words from it now present themselves to you, carrying new weight and giving the Psalm an entirely fresh emphasis. What's the new, prominent word? Could this be God's word to you now?

There is listening that occurs in relationships. We don't use the word "hark" anymore. As in "Hark! (Listen!) the herald angels sing." But if we harken to what is being said in relationships, this also is a way of listening to God. Like praying the Scriptures, this relational listening can become dialogue.

One witness to the power of listening is Frank Laubach, a Methodist missionary who went to the Philippines in 1930 to serve the Moros (Islamic island natives). He found an almost entirely illiterate people. Within seven years, half of the ninety thousand Moros tribespeople could read.

How did this happen?

Frank Laubach went on this mission alone, without his wife and small child. For a long, long time his only communication was prayer, and in that prayer he learned a remarkably effective method of adult literacy education. The method is listening, and it's used widely today in literacy programs all over the world.

God directed Laubach to listen to the language of the Moros in order to teach them.

"When you are teaching the Moros to read, your art is to say as little as you can and leave them to say as much as they will. Talk a great deal to me. Let others talk a great deal to you." This was what Frank Laubach understood God to say, and it opened up a vast pathway to human learning.

Listening is ultimately an act of love and trust. We seek to know and understand the difference in others, to understand their mystery.

To Live with the Spirit

To live with the Spirit of God is to be a listener.
It is to keep the vigil of mystery,
earthless and still.
One learns to catch the stirring of the Spirit,
strange as the wind's will.

The soul that walks where the wind of the Spirit blows
turns like a wandering weather-vane toward love.
It may lament like Job or Jeremiah,
echo the wounded heart, the mateless dove.
It may rejoice in spaciousness of meadow
that emulates the freedom of the sky.
Always it walks in waylessness, unknowing;
it has cast down forever from its hand
the compass of the whither and the why.

To live with the Spirit of God is to be a lover.
It is becoming love, and like to him
toward whom we strain with metaphors of creatures:
fire-sweep and water-rush and the wind's whim.
The soul is all activity, all silence;
and though it surges Godward to its goal,
it holds, as moving earth holds sleeping noonday,
the peace that is the listening of the soul.
—Jessica Powers

And in the context of living in the Spirit of God, Paul is out there ahead of us addressing our concern:

Who will separate us from the love of Christ?
Will hardship, or distress, or persecution,
or famine, or nakedness, or peril, or sword? . . .
I am convinced that neither death, nor life,
nor angels, nor rulers, nor things present,
nor things to come, nor powers,
nor height, nor depth,
nor anything else in all creation,
will be able to separate us
from the love of God in Christ Jesus our Lord.
—Romans 8:35, 38–39

Arthur writes:
I like an image of prayer drawn by the mystic, poet, and Anglican priest John Donne (1572–1631)—the entrance into the house (*John Donne: Selections from Divine Poems, Sermons and Devotions, and Prayers,* ed. John Booty, Paulist Press, Mahwah, NJ, 1990, p. 188). This is because being in prayer is like being inside a house, but a house with no walls, no boundaries. We are contained by the prayer; and we enter a familiar "place" by prayer, but a place limitless in scope. Here's what Donne said:

Prayer is our first entry, for when it is said,
"Ask and it shall be given," it is also said,
"Knock and it shall be opened,"
showing that by prayer our entrance is.

So there we are, across the threshold. Once a week, I telephone Beatrice O'Brien, my ninety-two-year-old mother-in-law and we say a decade of the rosary together. (She was my friend even before I met her daughter.) It doesn't matter where in the country she is at the time, which son or daughter she might be visiting. We have our routine.

We have a little chat, a sort of *Rune Before Prayer* in the Gaelic manner (for she's from Tipperary as was her husband, Maurice). We're in Donne's entrance hall.

The thing is though, once the rosary is under way, the first five beads are all to do with family and friends—we are in God's house of the mind, and we're mentioning the names who need a special word that day. There is no world except that house of prayer we've stepped into. It may be her ninety-year-old sister Peg in Ireland we're thinking of, or any of Beatrice's nine children and their spouses, or the twenty-five grandchildren or seventeen great-grandchildren. No sooner are they mentioned in prayer than there they are, in this house of prayer with us. It's not so much uncanny as heartwarming.

Rosary

Sometime the urge
is too great. I search
the tortuous back roads
until I find the solitude to
sit quietly in my truck with
my beads and my God. . . .

. . . and once there I sink
into a soft labial sibilance:
each bead round

and worn and wonderful
between thumb and finger;
each touch and tug pulling
me deeper into green
gardens of blossoming prayer,
into the mysterious heart
of my God.
—John E. Hopkins

As for our rosary duet, we've estimated that Beatrice has been saying the rosary for eighty-eight years. She sets the pace. We're Olympic class for speed and precision. I'm just into the final phrase of the first half of the Hail Mary—"blessed is the fruit of thy womb, Jesus"—and she's already into "Holy Mary Mother of God." As she reaches "now and at the hour of our death" I'm right in there again with "Hail Mary full of grace" to start all over again.

We're passing the baton as we finger the beads, rocking through the rosary, mantralike, both seeing different versions of the same thing. A eucharist of words. With the communion of saints, those we know and those we've known, gathered around us in this house without walls, without end. Amen.

There's one thing I particularly like. We're both from Europe. We both say "amongst"—as in "blessed art thou amongst women." Silly, isn't it? Yet it's so meaningful because it's familiar.

We want that relationship with Jesus and God, a relationship so meaningful because it's familiar. To create that familiarity means a frequency and regularity of relationship so that it is, like mine with Beatrice, most of all a friendship.

Yet there are moments for all of us when the immediate friendship isn't tangible. When we feel, and may indeed be, alone.

Gardening

By nightfall, my hands weep with blisters.
My arms are as heavy as the cartwheel
that must carry away the weeds.

I breathe in the night air, pull
at the roots of my existence.
Starting at the shed,

I walk circle within circle,
find prayer wheel after prayer wheel,
some broken, some still spinning,

though one, like a bell ringing,
sheep may safely graze.
Sheep may safely graze.

*

Lord, I seek your solace, your shadow.
Follow me in my chaos.
Bless my feeble attempts at prayer.

Bless the cartwheel that carries
the stone of my soul.
Though when graced, the stone

will make a wind sound
like a poem. Like a blossom
opening for the first time.
—Mary Ann Meade

7

Facing Fear with Contemplation

It isn't as if life is not full of miracles. It's more than that: It is miraculous, and anyone who stops taking it for granted will see that at once.

—Anthony de Mello, S.J.

Contemplation comes after the tears shed before God in prayer, after the pleading, after the offering of the world into God's light. It's then that comes the silence, the silence philosopher Max Picard spoke of as primal: "Before Genesis there was silence" (*World of Silence*, Henry Regnery Company, New York, 1952).

Dolores writes:

I think of contemplation as the wordless presence, simply abiding in God. Of course, it is also communion with the particular and with the universal.

Finally, in life, in reality, we stand, sit, kneel, bow, we are before the Presence, realizing at once our utter dependence on, and yet how much we are valued by, the One we call God.

As soon as my car turned onto the grounds of Weston Priory, a Benedictine priory in Vermont known for commitment to peace and justice, I felt the peace of creative hope and far-reaching love, of strong and inclusive community, of persistent prayer, all supported by the strong currents of contemplation. Stillness is in the air, the soil, in the simple chapel and the large barn where Sunday liturgy is celebrated. The dynamics or movements of the heart, mind, spirit, will, soul (of which we've been speaking) find their source and sustenance in contemplative living. This is what the Priory's life is all about; it's what our Christian life is ultimately all about.

The monks farm the land and they create beautiful works of art (pottery, woodwork, paintings), and they welcome strangers as Saint Benedict directed: "Receive all as Christ." Retreatants come for a few days or perhaps longer. For years, Weston Priory has been a sanctuary for Central American refugees who are amazingly integrated into the community. Sunday mornings, a thousand searching souls come to worship.

The homily used to be a dialogue of sorts. Since September 11, the monks simply invite the congregation to "be in silence," to let the power and majesty of God heal the wounds of those gathered in worship, and those far away, beyond the hillside steeped in prayer. On the Sunday seven weeks after the beginning of this age of fear, I shared with a thousand others the depth and truth and sanity of simply leaning on God, being conscious of my dependence on Providence, drawing on God's holiness to root out the fear and the violence that roams around within all of us. One of the poignant discoveries of that late October Sunday was that we—the sharers of stillness—were strangers no more.

There are moments in every life when awareness of God's abundant life and love breaks through. The birth of a child, a vista, the soaring wordless wonder of a Beethoven symphony—these windows give us glimpses of the glory of God's reality. It is possible, however, so the spiritual guides tell us, to retrain our consciousness so that we are not dependent on chance encounters to experience this ultimate unity.

We can practice contemplation, humbly and steadily, not as an end in itself, certainly not as an escape, but, for the purpose of conscious union with God, cross and all. The practice of contemplative prayer is to recognize in the deepest, most experiential way the truth that "In [God] we live and move and have our being" (Acts 17:28). Saint Paul preached this wondrous news to the Athenians and his words are instructive for this moment in our human history.

> *Athenians [or Americans, or Afghans, or . . .], I see how extremely religious you are in every way. For as I went through the city and looked carefully at the objects of your worship, I found among them an altar with the inscription, "To an unknown god." What therefore you worship as unknown, this I proclaim to you. The God who made the world and everything in it, he who is Lord of heaven and earth, does not live in shrines made by human hands, nor is he served by human hands, as though he needed anything, since he himself gives to all mortals life and breath and all things. From one ancestor he made all nations to inhabit the whole earth, and he allotted the times of their existence and the boundaries of the places where they would live, so that they would search for God and perhaps grope for him and find him—though indeed he is not far from each one of us. . . . Since we are God's offspring, we ought not to think that the deity is like gold, or silver, or stone, an image formed by the art and imagination of mortals.*
>
> —Acts 17:22–29

We come to this knowledge about the true state of things, namely that we all of every race and nation indwell—i.e., draw our life and meaning—from the same source, the Lord and God of all and that God is as close to us as our breath, through the development of contemplative awareness.

What does this mean?

The first, extremely important point is that contemplation is not reserved for monks, nuns, and hermits. Beatrice Bruteau, philosopher and writer of contemplative theology, defines contemplation as the shaping of a life, in the midst of bustle and busyness, of fears and challenges, in which we know that we do, indeed, live and move and have our being in the source of all love. She says that we know, existentially, that we are loved for the persons we are, and therefore we don't need to prove ourselves to God or to anyone else. We are, however, heavily conditioned to think, and to act, as if we must earn God's love, because we are somehow defective. So we strive and clutch and cling—afraid. To discover the truth, some reconditioning of consciousness is needed.

Bruteau is an excellent guide for helping one begin to develop a contemplative attitude toward life. She says the foundation is to learn to be still and open. This means, among many things, noticing our hardened hearts. The practice of stillness is to relax the tense and hardened inner self, which blocks us from hearing the voice of God, seeing the divine shadow, feeling the healing touch.

Her advice is sound and practical. She advises that we first relax the body, simply sitting still. She stresses that we must understand how our bodily and emotional states are intertwined, and how changing one piece of the equation can affect the whole. Bruteau uses the verb "taming" to describe the bodily practices. One needs to tame the body to keep it healthy and calm. A commitment to a balanced life is essential, and this includes judicious use of food, alcohol, and stimulants.

Stilling the whir inside the body may be more difficult and will require daily practice. And what exactly might such a practice look like? It will most certainly include creating an environ of external silence for some period each day: twenty minutes is considered the basic minimum. Twenty minutes. Hardly too high a price to pay for learning to focus the inner life.

The house is one of the classic symbols of one's inner world, and of the self. Dreams of houses that are messy, or cramped, or are growing often give the dreamer clues as to what is going on inside. The house is also a central symbol in mystical literature, Saint Teresa of Avila's seven mansions come to mind.

I sometimes turn to the following poem by Jessica Powers as I prepare for a period of meditative stillness and contemplative prayer.

The House at Rest

On a dark night
Kindled in love with yearnings—
Oh, happy chance!—
I went forth unobserved,
My house being now at rest.
—Saint John of the Cross

How does one hush one's house,
each proud possessive wall, each sighing rafter,
the rooms made restless with remembered laughter
or wounding echoes, the permissive doors,

the stairs that vacillate from up to down,
windows that bring in color and event
from countryside or town,
oppressive ceilings and complaining floors?

The house must first of all accept the night.
Let it erase the walls and their display,
impoverish the rooms till they are filled
with humble silences; let clocks be stilled
and all the selfish urgencies of day.

Midnight is not the time to greet a guest.
Caution the doors against both foes and friends,
and try to make the windows understand
their unimportance when the daylight ends.
Persuade the stairs to patience, and deny
the passages their aimless to and fro.
Virtue it is that puts a house at rest.
How well repaid that tenant is, how blest
who, when the call is heard,
is free to take his kindled heart and go.
—Jessica Powers

Just as there are many mansions in heaven, there are many doorways into the stillness that leads to awareness of the divine. Imaginative meditation focused on a scriptural passage, a method central to Ignatian and Carmelite spirituality, is one doorway. Another springs from the richness of *lectio divina.*

It is that *word* that leads us into the inner recesses of silent stillness. Practitioners of centering prayer are well versed in this method.

Whatever doorway is chosen, what awaits is the energy, the ongoing dynamic life of Jesus. Jesus lives. This is the foundation of our Christian faith. And we live in him, and he in us. Such astounding words! The practice of meditation and the concomitant contemplative way of being bring this reality into sharp clarity—clarity about ourselves, about the world, and about Christ.

Self-clarity allows us to see the "real person," not the "descriptive self." Bruteau writes:

> *Respect for life, in its understated form, recognizes this. Our sense of feeling good in being ourselves does not come from any kind of contrast or comparison with others. It comes directly and immediately out of our realization of being a creative act of God, simply unique and absolutely precious.*
>
> (*Radical Optimism*, Crossroads, New York, 1993, p. 68)

Furthermore, the contemplative is not passive in the face of cruelty and violence. Again, Bruteau elaborates: "I believe it is part of the contemplative's vocation to trace evil to its discoverable roots and find out how to deal with it effectively."

We hear a great deal these days about evil doers and evil deeds. Could it be possible that contemplative living can light our way to understanding that which is almost beyond comprehension? And isn't it true that deeper understanding leads to wiser decisions?

It has always been difficult for me to enter into the state that Ignatius calls "holy indifference," that is, to prefer God's will in all things. I stumble over the words that indicate I do not prefer health to sickness, wealth to poverty, and so on. I am being helped, however, by Bruteau and her explication about the way a contemplative behaves, and especially by some serious meditation on chapter 14 of Paul's letter to the Romans, which seems particularly suited to the present time. Saint Paul directs the Romans:

> *Welcome those who are weak in faith, but not for the purpose of quarreling over opinions. Some believe in eating anything, while the weak eat only vegetables. Those who eat must not despise those who abstain, and those who abstain must not pass judgment on those who eat; for God has welcomed them. . . . Some judge one day to be better than another, while others judge all days to be alike. Let all be fully convinced in their own minds. Those who observe the day, observe it in honor of the Lord. Also those who eat, eat in honor of the Lord, since they give thanks to God; while those who abstain, abstain in honor of the Lord and give thanks to God.*
>
> *We do not live to ourselves, and we do not die to ourselves. If we live, we live to the Lord, and if we die, we die to the Lord; so then, whether we live or whether we die, we are the Lord's.*
>
> —Romans 14:1–8

These common sense words of Paul are teaching me much about holy indifference, but they require consistent pondering to seep deep within where fear still has a hold.

We contemplate. But this doesn't stop the unbidden thought. To quell it, we rely on the five senses, waiting for one to banish the intruder. It is said that our sense of smell is the one best attuned to recalling childhood. Smell can certainly banish intruders.

Marigolds

I love marigolds
they smell like summer, not sweet
but pungent like sweat
and earthy things brought
to fruition through honest
toil and hard labor.
—Martha Wickham

Too often, the flitting, fleeting image (or nonimage) of death—or its mirror self, life—is what disturbs contemplation.

We cannot avoid the fact that catastrophe can befall us at any second. Nor can we avoid Paul Tillich's observation that "it is impossible for a finite being to stand naked anxiety for more than a flash of time."

What then, in God's name, are we to do? Please?

Ask for mercy.

To survive, we have to hand over our anxieties to God. But we don't know if we can do that.

To survive we have to embrace evil. And we don't know if we can do that.

To survive we have to accept our powerlessness.

Having looked at our faith, hope, and love, at our prayer and contemplation, is it possible that we have managed to accept our powerlessness?

If so, that's marvelous! The marvelous opening to God is powerlessness. Powerlessness plus contemplation equates to powerlessness plus emptiness.

Powerless and empty—this is how we hand over our anxieties. "My yoke is easy and my burden light." He's already told us where he is. Give him the burden. Unload, and be empty.

Our protection rests with God when we confess our weakness and our total dependence. Perhaps sin is nothing more than examples of us playing with power. The power of me exploiting, or dominating, or using my skill and wit, my greater strength and might. To momentarily oppress so I might gain my pleasure, my purpose, my material end. If I do any of this to my contemporaries I am doing it to those who can get me into heaven.

Paul Valliere is correct when he writes that those who would be followers of the Lamb "must engage with, suffer and be redeemed with their contemporaries." Just look at our contemporaries around the world. They are integral to our redemption.

If contemplation is a form of emptying, we are not just emptying ourselves of the world. We are emptying ourselves of our sin and, consequently, refilling ourselves with love—for neither God nor nature loves a vacuum—love for our contemporaries, and for God.

We don't comprehend. We reach for comprehension when we reach to touch the hem of that garment of nakedness we may never wear. In contemplation, though, we can reach for the garment again. At some point, it will come into our grasp. We can wear it when we've reached the fullness—that is, the emptiness.

Confiteor Deo

I will go to the altar of my God
wearing only the vestment of my skin.
I shall lift the loaf towards heaven one crumb
at a time—until the mysterious skirmish
between God and asparagus rests deep
in the last few drops of blood red wine.

Lift me, Jesus! Tell me you have great books
and grandmas in heaven, flood me with hymns,
give me celestial pillows to rest on,

and tell me poems bloom into existence
each time angels come among us. Dare I
pray the secrets waiting in the saint's stone?

I want to be a seed spun to perfection
instead of just a lump. Let my ego
go limp as death into a single word.
Let my soiled voice embrace the very wind
that began as the breath of life and let
me sing until I run out of confessions.
—Fredrick Zydek

Christopher Manes, philosopher of the environment, lawyer, and authority on medieval literature, has a nice story about life and death. He recounts how Bishop Paulinus (354–431) told the English pagan King Eadwin about life on earth. This life, said Paulinus, is a king seated in his hall in winter before the fire when "in flies a sparrow, which flutters through the hall, comes in through one door, and exits through the other. Lo, during the time the bird is within, he isn't touched by the storms of winter. But that lasts only a little while, a twinkling of an eye, before he soon returns to winter from winter. Just so this life of man appears only for a short time; what went before and what follows, we know not" (*Other Creations: Rediscovering the Spirituality of Animals*, Doubleday, New York, 1997, p. 9).

Ramage
(Sonnet for my Descendants)

In you, my blood will flow through unborn years
and dreams that danced down all my days
will shimmer in yours; salt of my tears
your lips will taste. In many ways

I will be with you. Sparks from my fire
your lives will set ablaze; from me, the root,
what astral-blossomed boughs may yet aspire,
what ancient flavors hide in future fruit?

So I shall live, some part of me survive
in other minds, our kinship to proclaim.
Seeds of my visioning will someday thrive—
new music to old runes. The very Name
that in my heart now jubilantly sings
will lift your souls upon transcendent wings.
—Sister Marion Storjohann, SS.CC.

Sister Marion entered religious life when she became a widow. She has four children, eleven grandchildren, and four great-grandchildren. She is looking down the ages—or at least the generations—and helps in seeing the continuity. The continuity that urges, drives us to embrace life with a fresh or renewed spirituality, the spirituality of life-to-be-lived. It's hard. We have been given life, even if life with pain, as others have relinquished life in pain. The great lure to persuade us to change and adapt and renew is the gift of the fact that we're still here. God may have bent lightning to keep us here.

Contemplating what our own life lived will mean to those who follow leads nowhere. We live on only if we've managed to put some love into a little pocket of someone else's heart, where its influence can linger for a surprisingly long time—even after our names are more or less forgotten. For the pocketed love can be pulled out like a handkerchief to wipe someone's tears long after we're dead. And that tearful someone will have been touched by love we deposited. It is a deposit the tearful can now draw upon to wipe someone's cares away. A deposit of love we put in place for others to use.

Otherwise, without our love pocket, in the normal course, that's it. By earthly measure, we're faded in three generations, gone in four.

Incredibly, it is by putting away a bit of love in the love pockets that we're touching here on earth what heaven is like. We're dealing in life beyond death. (And this is the only moment in our journeying together the topic of life beyond life is addressed.) Remember when we were looking at prayer, and John Donne suddenly had us standing in the entrance way to the house that is prayer? Well, our trying to think about heaven is not so far removed. We're on the outside, trying to look in. There are windows, but we're small and they're high up.

Prayer hasn't opened the door for us yet.

We don't know what heaven looks like but we'd appreciate a peek in. The love we give to others is like a little footstool. By standing on the footstool, because it quickly sinks into the soft moss of daily living again, we are able to take a fast glance through the window into heaven. When we know, through love, that we've connected with someone's life, when we know, through love, that someone has connected with ours, we've glimpse a bit of God. God and heaven and love and life beyond life are all the same thing.

This is where the trust element of love enters the equation. We're trusting God's Word—Jesus. We're trusting that if we love, we shall have life beyond life. This is God's side of the bargain. And to keep us interested, God lets us glimpse life-beyond-life, that is, we glimpse God through those full or fleeting moments of love.

In death and dying, Gaelic Christianity honored a person, a man or woman, known as a "soul-friend." As someone lay dying, this special person, the soul-friend, intoned a hymnlike prayer known as a "soul peace." At the moment of death, it was the duty of Saint Michael the Archangel to convey the soul to the abode of bliss. As the archangel of heaven and the archangel of hell face each other across the balance beam, the soul is weighed on the balance.

All we have, soul-naked before God, like makeweight on the good end of the balance beam, are the pockets of love we stored away in the nooks and crannies of other people's lives. What we learn through this is that the entry into heaven is an accompaniment. We are escorted from the balance beam.

Easy, isn't it? Of course it is, just as Sister Mary Virginia Micka, C.S.J., reminds us: "God IS," she writes, "but thrives on being ISN'T." In contemplation it all makes sense. Why does it make sense? Because we can accept it as part of the mystery. Having accepted it, a bit like a birthday gift we knew we were going to get, we can set it aside for opening later and continue the conversation with the giver—God, who prefers to confer in silence. Therefore, we contemplate in silence, God's preferred medium of exchange.

Then, the firestorm! In contemplation we're suddenly confronted again by those September 11 images. And we go through the cycle once more.

To quote the final lines of Sister Mary Virginia's poem "On Giving Up" is to hear again what's going on in our lives.

> *God IS but thrives on being ISN'T,*
> *And in just such terrifying*
> *nonaffirming ways as ours,*
> *who probe the dark, then stumble,*
> *then cry out in heaps of helplessness.*

Temporary heaps. A temporary helplessness. Though one that can invade even contemplation (just as it can invade life, which means prayer. For life is prayer.)

Temporary until we remind ourselves that faith is a gift, and the gift contains the challenge. Hope is how we answer the challenge. Love is why we answer it. We take a chance, and take a chance on people. We set the image in perspective. Retrieve the quiet calm, and give ourselves to the moment of our next interaction. We are vital to the next person we touch—we simply don't know why we're vital.

We don't know whom we touch. One hundred and sixty years ago a young Italian Passionist priest named Dominic Barbieri happened to be in England, and happened to be the one who received an Anglican priest named John Henry Newman into the Catholic Church. This priest became Cardinal John Henry Newman and his strengths, learning, and insights are still with us as guidance beyond tomorrow and tomorrow.

It is in living out our varied vocations we're connected, vine-like, to the people and places we touch. And sometimes it is the simplest thing we do that has the most impact. The overall impact of all Christians reaching out and touching can be enormous. Its potential is at the heart of so much that church leaders, writers, and teachers have striven for in recent decades. This need to gently but firmly touch the world with the best gifts we have to offer.

"Beware," warned the poet John Milton (1608–1674), "the fury of a patient man." Be warned, we'd add, the endurance of the Christian infused with quiet calm.

Contemplation has its own measure—as well as a place of honor in Christianity.

When Mount Carmel mystics sat in what was simply an orchard, when the desert fathers were not known beyond a radius of fifty miles, they had already discovered something that hasn't aged in two thousand years:

I love the feeling which, in former days,
Sent men to pray amid the desert's gloom,
Where hermits left a cell, or saints a tomb.
Good springs alike, from penitence and praise.
—Anonymous

Arthur writes:

The White Friars, the Carmelites, returned to the banks of the River Medway, to Allington Castle, three centuries after they had been driven from the same spot in Kent, England, by the forces of the Reformation. There was nothing remaining of the original monastery, a few walls now incorporated in outbuildings.

No memory of its former state,
No record of its fame,
A broken wall, a fallen tower,
A half-forgotten name;
A gloomy shadow on the wave,
And silence deep as in the grave.
—Anonymous

But casting a benevolent shadow over where the abbey had been was the still surviving and still occupied Allington Castle. In the late 1950s, the old friar laid his siege. He stopped by the castle one day and chatted with the owner. The friar asked if the owner would sell the castle to the friars, and the owner replied, reasonably enough, that it was and long had been his family's home. It wasn't for sale. The friar understood perfectly. He returned regularly to politely ask the same question, and to receive the same answer.

One year, changing the conversation a little, the owner said to the friar: "And how much would you pay for the castle?" The old friar, who knew little about property values, said oh, perhaps as much as five thousand pounds (worth at the time about $12,500). The owner was amused.

He sold the castle to the Carmelites. A huge and friendly pile, a welcoming sort of castle, with traces of the old moat, and enormously thick and tall wooden doors fit to keep out any unwanted. With a tiny door in one of the enormous doors to let in people who were wanted.

Once in the friars' possession, the castle was done over as a monastery and retreat center. All was ready. The Guinnesses of brewery fame helped with the costs, and with the wine cellar.

To celebrate, there was a magnificent banquet in the huge hall of the castle that started early with a grand, happy—and later, even happier—crowd of guests. There was laughter and song and reminiscence. But the monastery had set its rules in place. All revelry must stop at 10:00 P.M.! Which, with the wine cellar somewhat depleted, is what happened, that is, except for the little band who asked the abbot if they might leave the castle and repair to the pub on the opposite side of the canal. Ah, said the prior, a problem. We lock the little door at 10.30 P.M. That's the rule. But there's no rule about leaving the big doors open. When the little band returned at midnight, the creak of the huge door echoed along corridors and up winding stone staircases and into more corridors and turrets. Once inside, they realized what the sleeping castle was—a monastery.

The mysticism that is the only tangible element of contemplation, and barely tangible, except as a word, had sent its breath into every castle nook and cranny ahead of the creaking noise. At 5:00 A.M., the wakened sleepers had breathed in what mysticism itself had breathed out. Contemplation had settled.

Mysticism can be a soft, light shawl. As such it was evident on those present in the chapel, on those walking and praying on the grounds. Contemplation lay upon them like a light, warm blanket across chilly shoulders. Three centuries had passed. Yet, overnight, the contemplation was as much a part of the place as if it had never been ejected from the area.

The point is that this is what contemplation can be in our lives—something we place across the shoulders of our soul like a shawl. And once in the habit, the easier it becomes.

We should approach contemplation as something uninterruptible. Contemplation is not meant to be an interlude in our day or week or month. More fully explained, we should see the day and the week and the month as essential interruptions to our periods of contemplation.

To create this receptivity, we have to ease an opening into our lives and allow contemplation into it, to look ahead and determine moments that will be contemplative moments, even moments of "lightning contemplation."

Contemplation has to be strung out into the future like a never-ending single strand of rosary. A spiritual DNA double helix stretching toward eternity. Each moment intended for contemplation is spaced out like a bead—regular and frequent.

In this mystical monastery we can join the party that is life. We can wind down with a trip to the pub across the canal. We can sneak back in to the care of God by the big door. We can find the chapel-of-ease, the lee of the tree, the bench in the monastery garden, to do that one thing that will connect all of life, with all of life: contemplate.

Quiet Persistence

Outside my room is a quiet green bush
That deals in absolutes.
Each morn it opens up
Startling blood-red blooms,
Calling bees bumbling by.
And undulating hummingbirds,
Each wearing colorful working suits,
The Bee in Swiss-Guard colors,
The bird in iridescence.

Exhausted, each eve it closes down,
Folding up like a walking stick its blooms,
Awaiting the morn to try again.
How long will this go on, this stalking?

Until the bees buzz by,
The bobbing hummingbird sips with perky beak
Into the nectar-bed, rubbing life-preserving
Pollen off.

I doff my hat to this silent scene,
Morn and night, a delight.
Persistence pays.
The huge red flowers
Are bowers for bird and bee
But momentarily.
Can the bush renew itself
In such simple ways?
The Lord said to Paul,
"For in weakness
Power reaches perfection."
The burly bush
Depends on such a resurrection.
—Brother Remigius Bullinger

The lure of the outdoors, of creation, draws contemplation to it like a mother bird returning to its nest. Creation and contemplation nestle.

The day is now at dusk time:
Soft touches of evening quiet
Hush busy earlier hours
And tinge the air with peace.
Soon the sun, slowly setting,
Will leave a golden afterglow
Of whispering beauty
Before night's darkness falls.
Tranquil dusk.
—Sister Maria Corona Crumback, I.H.M.

If we have experienced quiet calm, we know what quiet calm is, we can plan for future quiet calm. Quite simply, the very planning induces calm—as does poetry—as we draw the calm of that future toward our present moment.

Simply by centering on the calm that is not yet, we envelop ourselves in it. This is almost as miraculous as life itself.

Contemplation is not only of the moment, it is soul memory, and soul anticipation.

Soul-memory contemplation does not exist in time and space; it is out of time and space. Past or future, experienced or anticipated, contemplation is always the same at the moment we accept it.

We can close our eyes for barely a moment or two and bring in, bring on everything that is contemplation. Eyes closed and listening to our breathing, we are back with the bush, or anticipating the garden or the cloister to come.

Lightning contemplation. Instant contemplation. Fear-banning contemplation. Momentary, and at hand. Not even a fumble for words for a prayer to go along with it.

Arthur writes:

Forty years ago I went into the New Jersey swamps to a secret spot that Hope Buyukmihci called "Unexpected Treasure." (She used the expression, too, as the title of her 1968 book [Evans & Co./Lippincott]). The refuge was an unexpected treasure to school children, who were invited to visit in small numbers. Two hundred and fifty acres of Hope's determination to save something that is, was, and ought to be against what the state of New Jersey was determined to become. Unexpected Treasure was a refuge for everything that lived naturally, normally, in the New Jersey pines. There was unexpected treasure of a different sort for me.

It was a key for me, a key to help me unlock that old

conundrum Jesus set before us that still returns to bug me until I deal with it: "Unless you are like little children . . ."

"Children," Hope said, and later wrote, "are naturally passionate. They have an innate capacity for being entranced. Their kind of childish rapture is closely akin to the sense of wonder that, in adult life, marks the artist and the creative scientist. It is sad that this marvelous freshness and intensity of childish feeling and perception so rarely survives the deadening educational progress or the many disillusionments which we lump together as 'growing up.'"

Hope herself had given me the key. Jesus is saying: unless you are like little children in "marvelous freshness and intensity."

To return to Brother Remigius's poem, contemplation provides the setting that opens the blooms of our own receptivity to the bumblebees of marvelous freshness and the hummingbirds of intensity.

Quietly calm.
Completely open.

Facing fear with?—Nothing, except each other.

Facing fear with?—Nothing of earthly value.

Facing fear with?—Everything that Jesus values, and everything life on earth and the earth itself values.

Facing fear with?—God of and in Creation, God of and in the Word.

The Word made flesh. The same flesh as ours.

Ours, unlike his, is timorous.

Timorous, yet questing.

Fearful.

Fear-filled.

Yet trusting.

Amen.

Acknowledgments

Atlanta Archbishop Paul J. Hallinan (1911–1968) appears in these pages several times. He was a key participant in the Second Vatican Council (1962–1965), especially on liturgical issues. But, more to the purpose here, he was a keen observer of the United States, and a prophet who spoke to America's promise, purpose, and problems. In six years, between 1962 and his untimely death in 1968, he delivered more than a hundred major addresses on issues ranging from testimony on behalf of Dr. Martin Luther King, Jr., to a tribute to Flannery O'Connor. He also penned a score of pastoral letters, hundreds of sermons, and other statements. A lively selection of the best of his writings is *Days of Hope and Promise*, edited by Vincent A. Yzermans, Liturgical Press, Collegeville, MN, 1973.

This book is quite dependent on poets. We thank so many of them for their inspiration, works and words. We formally acknowledge the following for their permission to reprint their works in this book:

Kevin Anderson, "Reflection on Mark 10:13–16"
Jeannie Bench, "Prayers of Beige"
Sister Janet Benish, O.C.V., "Insomnia"
Justine Buisson, "Mouse Tale"
Brother Remigius Bullinger, "Quiet Persistence"
Hope Sawyer Buyukmihci, "In April Once"
Sister Maria Corona Crumback, I.H.M., "Hidden Treasure"
Marilyn Cunin, "Thich Nhat Hanh and a 3-Hole Punch"
Margaret Doyle, "How Easily a Miracle"
Bob Dufford, S.J., O.C.P., "Be Not Afraid"
Kathleen Gunton, "Monody in a Time of Disaster"
John E. Hopkins, "Rosary"
Vic Hummert, "Pure Air," "Walking Humbly With God"
Nina Isabel Jennings, "The Latch-String to Happiness"
Sister Marion Storjohann, SS.C.C., "Ramage"
Dom Julian, O.S.B., "If Everything Is Lost"

Father Michael J. Kennedy, "Following Directions"

Leo Luke Marcello, "Reversals and Recent Acts of God," "God Who Knows the Cry of Pain, and Death," "Walking Through Paradise with a Friend Who Doesn't Believe"

Joseph W. Mayer, "Simple Faith"

Father Kilian McDonnell, O.S.B., "Perfection, Perfection"

Mary Ann Meade, "Gardening"

Father Augustine John Moore, "The Infant's Eyes"

Sascha T. Moore, "Liturgy"

Stella Nesanovich, "Trust"

Nancy J. Nowak, "Burning"

Dennis Queally, "Incense"

C. Richardson, "Flying in America"

Judith Robbins, "That the Bones You Have Crushed May Thrill"

Father Dan Rocheleau, "In the Light of My Father's Shadow"

Cheryl Sawyer, "One"

Sandra M. Schneiders, I.H.M., "Faith / Life"

M. Tufano, "Loud and Quiet"

Vineyard Press, for "Morning Prayer" and "Rune Before Prayer" from *Celtic Invocations*, (Alexander Carmichael)

Alice Ward, "Crossroads," "Me?"

John Sladen Whittle, "Exit 92B," "Patience"

Martha Wickham, "Marigolds"

Fredrick Zydek, "Confiteor Deo"

Sister Mary Virginia, "On Giving Up"

There are brief poems by Sheldon and Jean Vanauken, now both deceased, from their book *A Severe Mercy*, Harper & Row; quotations by Archbishop Paul Hallinan, excerpted with permission from Vincent Yzermans' *Days of Hope and Promise*, Liturgical Press; lines suggested by Hope Sawyer Buyukmihci in her book, *Unexpected Treasure* TK; and the Annie Sullivan incident from Robert McClory's *Faithful Dissent*.

Arthur writes: "My debt to two sources of constant inspiration, Alexander Carmichael's *Celtic Invocations*, and Carmelite Sister Wendy Beckett's *The Gaze of Love* (Harper Collins), cannot be overstressed. And always worthy of mention as a spiritual starting are the words of Anthony de Mello, S.J.

Dolores writes: Evelyn Underhill (d. 1941), an Anglican English laywoman who many believe to be one of the twentieth century's most astute writers of the mystical life in the secular world, was a prolific writer and respected throughout Europe. She is one of the most profound influences on my own life and her book *Practical Mysticism* (Dover Publications, Mineola, NY, 2000) is a cherished part of my personal library.

Another writer I hold in high esteem is Jessica Powers and six of her works appear in this volume: "If You Have Nothing," "Intimation of Doom," "The House at Rest," "The Mercy of God," "To Live with the Spirit," and "The Rag Man." These are all reproduced from *The Selected Poetry of Jessica Powers*, ed. Regina Siegfried, A.S.C., and Robert F. Morneau, ICS Publications, Washington DC, 1999 by permission of Mother of God Carmel in Pewaukee, Wisconsin, except for the previously unpublished "Intimations of Doom," which appeared first in my own *Winter Music: A Life of Jessica Powers, Poet, Nun, Woman of the 20th Century*, Theological Book Service, 1992.

Other reading: Michael Ford's *Wounded Prophet: A Portrait of Henri J. M. Nouwen* (Doubleday, New York, 1999)

Christopher Manes's *Other Creations: Rediscovering the Spirituality of Animals* (Doubleday, New York)

We offer a bow and a curtsy to John Sprague of Thomas More Publishing who took this book under his wing on a prayer that we'd get it done in six weeks; and for his careful editing of a hurried manuscript. We both wish to thank our spouses for once more accepting our distractedness and preoccupation during the period the book was being written (and at others times, too!). And we acknowledge the work of our agent, Robert Ducas.